DATE DUE

LONE JOURNEY

other books by
JEANETTE EATON

LEADER BY DESTINY
NARCISSA WHITMAN

LONE JOURNEY

THE LIFE OF ROGER WILLIAMS

by JEANETTE EATON

ILLUSTRATED BY WOODI ISHMAEL

HARCOURT, BRACE AND COMPANY
NEW YORK

PRINTED IN THE UNITED STATES OF AMERICA

To
WINIFRED KITTREDGE EATON
and
WEBSTER WRIGHT EATON
Heirs of New England's Finest Tradition

LONE JOURNEY

1

"HO there! Roger!"

Lustily the urchin shouted up at a boy framed in the window of a half-timbered brick house. The shout was answered by an eager smile, a nod, and a quick wave of the hand. Immediately the boy inside began closing the heavy shutters, hiding from view a sign in handsome letters which read, "James Williams, Merchant Taylor." In another moment a small figure in furred cape and long red stockings came dashing down the steps.

"I had to mind the shop this hour," he explained. "All my father's apprentices went with him to the Guildhall to prepare for the feast."

"Make haste now!" cried the other boy impatiently. "The procession will soon pass Cow Lane!"

The pair raced down the street between small houses of brick and past a stone mansion set within a garden. Their buckled shoes kicked up dust or clumped through mud. Their big velvet caps teetered on their long curls. Panting, they reached Lamb's Conduit at the end of the lane. At this place where horses and cows were watered, where women came to fill their pitchers for laundry tubs, loafers and gossips were always gathered. But this afternoon there was a huge crowd of young and old with many women among them pushing and chattering.

As he ducked skillfully under brawny arms and billowing cloaks, Roger lost his companion. No matter! Here he was at the very front of the crowd and now the pipes, drums, and trumpets could be heard coming along Cheapside.

A young fellow in a soiled purple doublet good-humoredly stood back to give the boy more room. "Be ye not the son of Williams, merchant tailor?" he asked. Receiving a smiling "Yes, good sir," the man went on, "Perchance you know if the King leads the Earl and Countess today to the feast of the merchant tailors?"

Roger shook his head. "Nay, sir, King James was to attend the wedding and then speed the bride and bridegroom on their way."

"Look, masters!" shrieked a woman's voice. "They come—the guards and horsemen!"

Carrying halberds and bearing the colors of the Earl, a company of royal guards marched along in the direction of Snow Hill. Close on their heels walked the trumpeters in slashed doublets and purple hose. A brave show of horsemen followed on dancing steeds with rosettes on their bridles. Behind them rolled and bumped a handsome coach drawn by four black horses and the crowd began to cheer. "Hats off to the Lord Mayor!" "Make way for the Lord Mayor of London!"

Trumpets from another marching section drowned the cheers. And now at last appeared the huge open carriage magnificently gilded and furnished with coachman and lackeys in livery. Seated side by side among piled cushions, gorgeous in satin, velvet, and fine ruffs of lace, sat the pair for whom all London had turned out.

"Huzzah, the Earl of Somerset!" "Long live the Countess!"

So rose the scattered cries into the foggy air. Never was handsomer groom than this one and never more beautiful bride. The smiling couple nodded and waved. Slowly amid floating banners and the dimming sound of trumpets the procession wound its way toward the great Guildhall.

To Roger's amazement the mood of the crowd changed at once. "No luck will come with this stolen bride!" sneered a woman's voice.

"Fair faces do not make fair deeds," growled a man near Roger.

"Nay, truly," cried another, "this favorite of the King, this Earl of Somerset, spends without stint from a purse we poor folk must fill!"

In the midst of a chorus of angry "Ayes!" a bass voice sang out, "There passed our Parliament! 'Tis the Earl who makes the laws!"

An instant later Roger was more astonished still. Someone at the far edge of the crowd yelled, "God save good King James!" But the surly crowd made no response and with discontented mutters began to scatter in a dozen different directions.

What was wrong? Roger strolled up Gilt Spur street in great perplexity. He thought all British subjects except the Puritans cheered the monarch. Hadn't he been sternly taught that everyone must honor James the First? Why did the crowd say hateful things against the splendid bride and groom? That at least his father might explain when he came back from the wedding feast.

Suddenly Roger stopped dead. In a little while his feet would have carried him to Smithfield, that open meadow where he had vowed he would never go again. He looked toward Pie Corner and thought regretfully of the good times he had once had when his elder brother took him to Smithfield. It lay on the far side of the fashionable suburb, Snow Hill, outside the walls of London. At the northern end of the huge tract horse and cattle sales took place. Football games were played there by burly young sports. Sometimes open air plays were given with a horrid devil standing at the mouth of a smoking hell. Best of all were the fairs with sweetmeat booths, fortune tellers, roasting pigs, and puppet shows.

Then two years ago something happened at Smithfield to make the place forever cursed to Roger. Stamped upon his memory were the sound and smell of a horror which broke in on his childhood play one sunny afternoon. Past the merchant tailor's house sped crowds of people fleeing from Smithfield. Some were sobbing, some crying out terrible oaths and shaking fists in air. Behind them far away a pillar of smoke rose toward the sky, and the breeze brought a dreadful stench not like any other odor the boy had ever smelled. Shaking with fright, he had run into the house and flung himself upon his mother. What were these people running from? What was the fire there on Smithfield? His mother tried to put him off, but he clung to her skirts and cried that he must know.

With tight, grim lips, she answered then, "A wicked Puritan is being put to death."

The boy fell back from his mother. Staring at her, he took in the dreadful truth. A human being, a living person, was being burned to death and crowds had come to see. "What might that be—a Puritan?" he gasped.

With pity for him in her eyes, but in a cold, stern voice, Mrs. Williams replied, "My son, a Puritan doth not believe in the great

Church of England, will not use the Prayer Book nor obey the Bishop. That is an evil person, be it man or woman."

Still trembling with shock, the little boy whispered fearfully, "Does a Puritan worship the Devil then?"

Impatiently Mrs. Williams pushed aside her embroidery frame and leaned forward. "Thou art too young to understand these things. I cannot say that Puritans worship the Devil, for they claim Christ as their own. But they disobey the King. We must all worship in the same fashion or England and the Church are undone."

For a long moment the child was silent. Then anger lighted up his face and glowed in his great, dark eyes. "It is a Christian they are burning at Smithfield!" he screamed. "The King is wicked to order this. I hate him!"

Later Roger wondered, remembering the look on his mother's face. For there was fear in it as well as anger. She put him supperless to bed that night and for two days he was not allowed to play with his ball or blow his penny whistle. Alone in his small, dark room he was given the Bible for his sole companion. He was glad of that. Except for his lesson books this was the only book he had ever had to read. He loved the wonderful stories in it and the poetry and the grand heroes like Daniel and David. During those days of punishment, however, it was the New Testament over which he pored. Perhaps it would tell him that the King was right to put the Puritans to death. If so, he would promise his parents he would try not to hate King James any more.

But when at last his father came to demand a confession of wrongdoing, Roger read aloud verses he had found:

9

"I am come a light unto the world that whosoever believeth on me may not abide in darkness."

"And I say unto you, everyone who shall confess me before men, him shall the Son of Man confess before the angels of God."

Roger looked up with one finger in the big book. "Do not these words mean, Father, that Christ loves the Puritans who believe on him, and therefore should the King not love them too?"

Mr. Williams glared at his small son. This was not repentance. This was unheard-of independence. And from a mere child! "Wilt thou become a Puritan, too?" roared the man.

For daring to argue with his elders Roger was soundly beaten. But deep in his heart he knew that his father had no answer for him except blows.

Never since that time had the boy set foot on Smithfield. As the whole bitter experience rose up before him now, he turned about in the direction of home. But in a moment he saw something which made him quicken his step. In the open square near the church of St. Sepulchre a number of boys were having a jousting match.

As he drew near, one of the group called out, "Roger Williams! Come, wilt thou play at jousting with us?"

Roger saw some of the others lower their staves. Several voices urged him to join the game. He said, smiling, "Nay, I have no skill at this. 'Tis a pity. But give me leave to watch for a while."

"You cannot joust?" cried one boy in surprise. "Dost thou play at tennis then?"

Roger shook his head. "That is a game for rich men's sons," he replied.

"How now?" asked a third lad. "What canst thou do?"

Roger laughed. "Not much to match thy muscles. I play a little on the lute."

"Pay him no heed," growled a tall fellow. "I know well this Roger Williams. His head is always in a book."

"Then," roared another jouster, lifting his wooden weapon threateningly, "we might well break it open to see what is inside."

Many a head was broken for less cause in these rough London days. Police there were none and everyone went about at his own risk. Roger knew this well. But grinning up at his big tormentor, he said, "It would pay thee ill to break this pate of mine. I have, alas, little learning in it yet."

Closer about the small figure pushed the circle of oafs. "Perchance thou dost like bear-baiting!" sneered a scornful voice.

"Aye, or cockfighting!" echoed the boy who had first called out to Roger.

"Nay, truly," he answered in a big, firm voice, "I like not baiting of any sort—be it of animals or men, and think it only cowards who do so. But hark ye all! This one thing I can do by way of sportive exercise and will do it my best for your pleasure. Stand back a way! Nay, farther yet!"

Impressed by the little chap's nerve and curious as to his intention, the big boys obeyed and moved far back from him. "Now watch!" cried Roger.

With a quick whirl, he bolted from the court like a hare and ran down the street. Only for a moment did he hear shouts and steps behind him. At top speed he raced on until, breathless, he leaped up the steps of his house. Then, with his hand on the brass door-knob, he looked about. Nobody was in sight. The boys had not thought it worth while to pursue him. Pleased with the success of his trick, he pushed open the door.

Roger's wish that his father would talk about events that evening came true. Returning from the bridal feast full of good wine and food, the merchant tailor was ready for conversation. First he declared that if ever woman's beauty explained wrongdoing it was that of the Countess of Somerset. Roger learned then that this fine lady had been married to another great Earl, but had fallen in love with a young Scotsman whom James First had brought down to his court. Robert Carr was his name and he had become a power in the realm through the King's great favor. First he was made a Lord and given large sums of money to spend. Then he was chief adviser to the King. When James learned that the Countess was in love with his favorite, he did everything he could to have her granted a divorce and made Robert Carr Earl of Somerset to accord with her rank. Many bishops and churchmen were against giving a divorce, but they were not firm enough to stand against the King. The husband of the Countess was sent abroad, she was set free of her marriage bonds, and in high glee James planned a gorgeous wedding for his handsome counselor in chief.

"The Lord Mayor told us tonight," said Mr. Williams, sweeping a look around the family circle to be sure everyone was listening, "that a wonderful masque had been given for the couple in the King's palace of Whitehall. Lord Chancellor, Francis Bacon, spent two thousand pounds to hire the best players and musicians and for costumes and scenery. Old Ben Jonson himself wrote the wedding song."

" 'Tis for this I am taxed for my property and thou for thy goods!" cried Mrs. Williams angrily.

"And for the wines to serve the courtiers and the King," growled her husband. "Many of the Earl's party arrived at the Guildhall so filled with wine that they fell upon the floor. Much evil goes on at Whitehall these days!"

Roger, with sharp remembrance of being punished because he had once cried out his hatred of the King, was astonished at this talk. "Today," he ventured to remark, "the watchers on the street would not cheer the King."

"And they never will," shouted his father, "until he call back Parliament. To tax the people without Parliament's consent is lawless and offends all but the King's minions. For two years he has ruled alone. Now begins 1614 and we wait to see if he will call Parliament again."

By this time Mrs. Williams was yawning sleepily. The oldest boy was moving chessmen about the board. Only Roger listened with keen interest. He asked if the King did not get his power from the people.

A sharp glance fixed him. "Our bishops and many others say the King rules by divine right from God," muttered the merchant tailor. Then he leaned toward his youngest listener. "But let me tell you this, lad, there is one man at Court who dares say otherwise. Sir Edward Coke, Chief Justice of the King's Bench, declares that King James himself must abide by the laws of England."

"Sir Edward Coke, my husband?" echoed Mrs. Williams. She had risen to put an end to the talk and was lighting her bedside candle. "That is the great man of law who attends service at St. Sepulchre. Often have I seen him descend from his fine carriage to enter the church."

"Oh, Mother!" cried Roger. "Show him to me when next we go to service in the church. I would see the man who says the law is above the King!"

Roger had his wish and far more. Five years later, when he was sixteen, this famous man was to offer him such amazing opportunities as to change the course of his entire life.

The Shorthand of Roger Williams

2

HAST thou donned a clean neck-band, Roger?"

Mrs. Williams held up a candle to scan the tall, handsome boy who had entered her bedroom to bid her a dutiful good-by.

"That I have, Mother, and have brushed my tunic well."

"Good." Then she heaved a deep sigh. "How I wish thou wert not garbed so soberly. Thy patron might like thee better for a touch of brightness."

"Not he, Mother." Roger frowned impatiently. Clapping the cloth bag slung over his shoulder, he said with an effort to be

15

pleasant, "So long as I have my notebook, inkhorn, and pen,
Sir Edward will think nought of my dress."

"Well, boy, I am glad thou hast learned this new fashion of
taking notes. Had all thy decisions been as wise, thou might go
far in this world."

"Farewell, Mother!"

Snatching up his candle, the boy strode out of the room and
down the dark stairs. In the hall a sleepy maid shot back the bolts
of the front door and repaid his thanks with a sulky look of disapproval. Drawing his woolen cape closely about him, he stepped
out to find that the gray of early morning was changing to light.

Roger's rapid pace along the dim streets was like the whirl of
his thoughts. Would his mother never accept the fact that his beliefs could not be shaken by blows or punishments or such sneers
as she had just uttered? It was no easy thing to be a dissenter. His
family had all been against him ever since he had become a Puritan. Even the servants seemed hostile.

But, thank Heaven, Sir Edward Coke did not share this view.
Many of the men whom the lawyer admired most were Puritans.
What luck to be in his employ! Sir Edward had seemed to like
him from the first, and when he learned that Roger could write
a kind of shorthand, he tried out the boy's skill at once. This
morning, after a month's testing, he was attending his patron at
the Star Chamber. But joy in his success could not prevent shrinking at the thought of crossing the threshold of this dreaded court.
All his life he had heard tales of its mock justice. It had been
made a means of ridding the King of all his enemies by a panto-
mime of law.

Fast walking had brought him to Ludgate Hill. He always

paused at the top of the incline to sniff the damp air as if it carried the very spirit of the city. Near by in the misty dawn rose the Gothic spires of old St. Paul's where now the great dome lifts. Down a cross lane he could see the River Thames. Here he could feel the shape of the sprawling town.

Eastward at the river's edge bulked the massive Tower of London. To the west above the river's deep curve were grouped those mighty structures which sheltered the heart and brain of England. First, the vast palace of Whitehall, town residence of the royal family. Beyond the palace yard stood Westminster Abbey, built and rebuilt for six hundred years. Joined to it was the Palace of Westminster, used mainly for Parliament and the high courts of law. On that February morning of 1619 London seemed a place of wonderful adventure to the dreaming eyes of a boy.

As Roger walked toward Sir Edward Coke's mansion the city began to wake up. Milk carts and drays rattled over the streets and already shopkeepers were taking down their shutters. But Roger's thoughts were upon his employer and the great book on law which he was writing. Some day, the author said, it would help the common man receive justice in the courts.

It was nearly seven when a lackey ushered the boy into the master's study. In furred dressing gown, with a peaked cap on his head, the lawyer was busy at a desk piled high with papers. Keen blue eyes and rosy cheeks denied the age suggested by white hair and beard. His voice boomed a welcome.

"Good morning to you, Master Williams. Prithee pull the bell cord by the door. We shall have breakfast now."

He did not look up again until one of the serving men who spread a table by the fire announced that all was ready. "Good."

Sir Edward laid down his quill, strode to the table and motioned his guest to sit. "Here is *parvum, sed bonum,* Master Roger."

Hungry after his brisk walk, the boy began to eat his bacon. But after a sip or two of milk, his host burst into talk.

"My work this morning brings up those past days when I served the good Queen. Then the English people had a voice in the government. The 'Crown in Parliament,' as we say, served the realm as two wings do a bird. But now one wing is folded. King James would rule without curb from Parliament. He even thinks any royal proclamation is a law and liked it not when I told him plainly such was not the case."

Carefully the speaker spread a slice of bread and butter. Then he asked abruptly, "My young friend, can you name the three parts of English law?"

Roger set down his pewter cup of milk. "Why, sir, ah . . . a bill passed by Parliament and signed by the King is law, sir, is it not?"

"Aye, it is Statute Law. But our most precious jewel is Common Law."

Roger listened thoughtfully. "Does that mean custom?"

Sir Edward beamed. "Nay, but well said all the same. Custom is the third kind of law. Common Law is more than custom. It hath grown up slowly as Justices throughout the land decided what was the right in a dispute or as they punished a wrong. It is these decisions I now set down in a book for general guidance."

As the old man fell to eating his eggs, Roger chuckled silently. He had just rememberd what his godfather, Squire Pemberton, had said when Roger on a visit to his farm had told about his new employment. "Pray God, lad, thou can bear with Sir Edward

Coke's eternal show of learning."

But it was fascinating to learn what was going on. "Sir Edward," he asked, "why are the merchant tailors sore angry because King James will not fight for Protestants abroad?"

The question turned on a stream of talk lasting while a servant dressed the lawyer for appearance at Court. Roger learned that the Protestant countries in Europe were at war with all the Catholic rulers. The whole British nation wanted to go to the rescue of the Protestant forces. But James preferred to appease Spain, in spite of its being such a strong Catholic power.

"Indeed," concluded Sir Edward, "it is whispered that the King's Councilor, Lord Villiers, would have Prince Charles wed the Spanish Infanta."

By this time the two were driving to Westminster in the lawyer's fine coach. Roger had been watching the barges on the river. But at this bit of gossip he turned around. Well he knew that a young man named Villiers had become the King's favorite in place of the Earl of Somerset. That personage, whom the boy had seen on his festive wedding day, had disappeared in a cloud of disgrace. Immediately the clever and ambitious Villiers had been given the post of Councilor and an Earl's title. People said he was fabulously wealthy.

"Tell me, sir," said Roger, "is Lord Villiers as powerful at Court as was the Earl of Somerset?"

"More powerful," replied Sir Edward in his loud voice. "He is the best friend of the Prince of Wales and rules the mind of the King."

As the coach stopped, a footman sprang down to open the door. Roger followed his patron into Westminster Hall with a deep throb of curiosity. Would he ever have a chance to see this Villiers who ruled behind the Crown?

Never before had the young Londoner stepped into the vast Hall, the only part of the palace left to modern times. His eyes sprang upward to the magnificent lacy arches of oak supporting the wooden roof. Below, tradesmen's booths lined the walls on each side of the noble structure. Men in every type of garb stood in groups about the paved floor.

Sir Edward strode to a door at the left protected by two guards with halberds. Instantly they stood aside for him and, with a curious look, let the youth with paper and inkhorn pass also. So did the doorkeeper on the other side of the portal. One glance about the famous room told Roger how the Star Chamber got its name. Gleaming stars were wonderfully painted on the ceiling.

At first the boy from Cow Lane felt as if he were sitting at a play. In splendid robes of crimson trimmed with ermine, the members of the Council ranged themselves on benches of carved oak. Hardly less gorgeous were the King's Judges placed opposite. By contrast the clerks and scribes seated at one end of the room looked sober as their tasks.

As Court opened Roger found his heart beginning to pound. Would some victim of the King be tried this morning? For an instant he glared at the judges, thinking, "Evil in ermine!" But as Sir Edward Coke arose to start his plea, the boy snatched up his quill and spread his papers out. It took his entire attention to follow Coke's speeches and retorts. Not until late afternoon, when he had made a fair copy of his notes, did he have time to reflect on what he had seen and heard.

There was no denying it was exciting to be behind the scenes of government. But he felt guilty to be at work in such a place. Next day he asked Sir Edward the question which most troubled him. The distinguished lawyers pointed out to him—the legal scholar, John Selden, and the brilliant Sir John Eliot, to say nothing of Sir Edward himself—how could they bear to plead in the Star Chamber? Wasn't that conniving with evil practice?

For an instant Coke's face grew rigid with anger. Then his eyes softened as if he pitied youth for its ideals and lack of knowledge of the world. His voice was gentle as he answered.

"Naturally, lad, a lawyer must earn his way, and the clients we defend before this court pay well. That is the meanest part of the truth. But there is more. His Majesty likes not to fling an enemy in prison without trial of any kind. Often a good lawyer can pile up so much evidence in his defense that even the King's Judges cannot stomach conviction. Remember also, my young censor, that often a really guilty man is tried in the Star Chamber. Many a villain have I had quaking before me there."

Roger bowed. "Yes, Sir Edward. But—oh, sir, it is a wicked place. It knows not your Common Law, nay, nor justice either." The boy was panting with emotion.

Coke nodded gravely. " 'Tis God's truth. Some day the Star Chamber must be abolished."

Weeks passed before Roger's curiosity about the King's Councilor was satisfied. But one day as the Court broke up in a general stir and talk, a sudden hush came over the room and all eyes turned in one direction. Through an inner door leading to the palace a figure had just entered. Instantly Roger guessed that this was the favorite, Lord Villiers, who "ruled the mind of the King."

Tall, slim, and broad shouldered, he stood outlined against the dark paneling. His claret velvet costume had fine lace ruffles at neck and wrist. One hand fingered a long chain of diamonds. The other imperiously beckoned one of the important nobles on the Council. Then Villiers turned his head with its long burnished curls to gaze haughtily about, and Roger caught a full view of his face. Handsome it was, but one more filled with disdain could hardly be imagined.

In his ear Roger heard a sharp whisper and whirled to find Sir Edward beside him. "There you see the most expensive item on the account books of the realm! Aye, boy, and the greatest foe of liberty!"

One morning Coke had a new task for his assistant. The lawyer had been summoned to an audience room in the palace for a brief questioning by the Chamberlain. Such was the crowd of perfumed courtiers in the apartment that only on leaving did Roger catch a glimpse of royalty. Suddenly, there he was, the King of England. A loose-jointed, homely man, guffawing loudly with a portly bishop!

Just at that instant the King's small eyes fixed on the staring youth. "And who might thee be?" he asked in a voice weighted with Scottish accent.

When Roger, with a deep bow, managed to stammer that he was Sir Edward Coke's shorthand writer, the King looked interested. "Know ye some Latin?" he inquired. Without waiting for an answer, King James burst into swift speech in the ancient Roman tongue.

"Sire," interrupted a musical voice, "Archbishop Laud desires a word with Your Majesty."

It was Prince Charles who spoke. His cool dignity and comely features gave him a far more regal air than that of his father. Roger longed to see the Archbishop, known to all as a fierce enemy of Puritans. But Sir Edward made a sign to him to leave.

On the palace stairs the two encountered another celebrated person. An elderly man was coming up as they went down. He greeted Coke with a frigid bow and as soon as he had disappeared around the stairway's turn, Sir Edward murmured, "The Lord Chancellor! No friend of mine at any time."

Roger knew that this was Francis Bacon. But not until much later did he learn that the man was a genius. Time hands Bacon down as the great man of his day, the writer of gem-like essays and founder of modern science.

None of these encounters, which any boy of his age would have envied, soothed the ache in Roger's heart. Those cases in the Star Chamber, so often lost before they could be defended! Frightened men shrinking before the judges in their ermine. Men doomed for no worse crime than refusing to disobey the law at the King's request. Even the guilty seemed mere pitiable victims of a court which disregarded honor. Sometimes at night Roger saw strained, white faces around his bed and he would pray that the Angel of the Lord might strike down that chamber of horrors with its ceiling of bright stars.

Sir Edward often remarked that the boy's cheeks were pale. "You work too hard, mayhap. But soon it will be summer and then you will come down to Stoke to help me with my book and breathe good country air."

Often had Roger heard his patron mention the country estate outside the village of Stoke Poges. But the first sight of the great house with its lawns and ancient trees and flower gardens took

his breath away. Never had he imagined such magnificent fur-
nishings. At his first dinner he could hardly eat for gazing at the
burnished silver. Yet he knew he was tasting the finest wines and
the most daintily cooked food.

Showing him into the paneled library filled with a superb col-
lection of books, his host said, "Early in the morning I am here
and shall expect you to be ready by seven."

That was a household all astir at dawn. Often Roger joined the
two married sons for a gallop over the meadows before breakfast.
"Slug-a-beds are we!" they would laugh. "Father has been writing for two hours."

As summer progressed so did the friendship between the old
man and the boy. Coke seemed to like to have Roger join the
circle of visitors who perpetually dropped in to discuss the questions of the day. Church reform and the restoration of Parliament
were the favorite themes.

John Hampden's visit was the most memorable. Wealthy and
distinguished, this young man was possessed of a patriotism which
was to make him famous in history. He had ridden over from his
beautiful estate in the Chiltern hills. With him came his cousin,
Edward Whalley, a clever-looking boy, younger than Roger.

Everyone agreed that day about the King's need to summon
Parliament. He had to have money and would call that body to
provide it. Both Coke and Hampden declared that when he did
so each would stand for election.

Across the dreamy look in Hampden's dark face passed a flash
of enthusiasm. "Thank Heaven for the House of Commons. The
nation's only hope of righting grievances. The House of Lords
follows the King's will too slavishly."

"So doth the Lord Chancellor," piped up Edward Whalley. "King James allows him to take large sums of money to push court cases."

Coke tugged angrily at his white beard. "True. At the next Parliament he should be tried at the bar of the Lords."

With quiet scorn Hampden summed it up. "Lord Bacon's receipt of bribes is in tune with a disgraceful reign."

Such talk gave Roger intimate knowledge of the results of unchecked power. At Sir Edward's he also learned many personal things such as good manners and a pleasing speech. But there came a time when his powerful friend decided that the gifted youth should have more formal education.

One afternoon when they were again in London, the attorney sent for Roger. "Know you the Sutton Hospital and School north of Smithfield?" he asked.

"Yes, Sir Edward. It is not far from my father's house."

He knew that his patron had persuaded Thomas Sutton to will part of his property to found a school for poor boys. Once Roger had slipped through the gate under its pointed archway and strolled past the red brick buildings into a lovely garden. This, a caretaker told him, had been planted by monks when the place was a Carthusian monastery.

"Perchance you have heard," went on Sir Edward, "that Archbishop Laud is one of the school governors. Yet for my aid in the founding of the school and as its High Steward, I top the Archbishop in influence." With a smile, he placed his hand on the boy's arm. "To come to the heart of the matter, Master Roger, I have a scholarship for you at Sutton's Hospital."

Roger leaned back to stare in unbelief. Then his face flushed with joy. "Oh, sir, in very truth? Such kindness—it exceeds every-thing!"

"Ah," muttered the old man with a pleased laugh, "your in-dustry at lessons must exceed my kindness, else it is undone."

It was easy for Roger, who loved study, to fulfill that obliga-tion. His swift progress in Latin and Greek revealed a gift for languages and he liked logic. Older and more experienced than most of the boys, he took small interest in their games and spent play time with his books. Even his one friendship with Richard Crashaw, destined to become a noted poet, was marred by a major disagreement.

News of a visit from Archbishop Laud was announced one morning at the school. Meeting Roger in the garden, Richard ex-pressed delighted excitement over the prospect.

Anger blazed in Roger's face. "Know ye not," he said sternly, "that this Archbishop is one who persecutes the Puritans?" A shudder ran through him as he thought of the burning pile on Smithfield. "Call ye that Christian?"

Richard would hear nothing against the famous churchman. Next day, when the prelate preached in chapel, Roger watched his friend lifting a radiant face to drink in every word. To the youthful Puritan, however, the sermon seemed hypocrisy and he scorned all who thought otherwise. Reluctantly he took his place among the older boys to be presented after chapel to the Arch-bishop.

Laud was small and round of shape. His red face, quick, bird-like glance, and cheerful manner gave no hint of the tyrant he was to become. Yet Roger's hating eyes found a cruel stubborn-ness in the thin lips and an utter lack of nobility in his presence.

To himself the boy thought, "This man is my earthly enemy."

He delighted Sir Edward Coke by his impression of the Archbishop. The lawyer was busier than ever these days. Still in Parliament, he was helping launch a program for church reform and had vigorously attacked the trade monopolies. These were sold for large sums by King James to a favored few among the merchants and resulted in high prices for all. Due mainly to Coke's efforts the evil practice was finally outlawed.

When Roger inquired about the trial of Francis Bacon, Coke said, "The Chancellor frankly confessed to taking bribes and abased himself. His Majesty has banished him from Court. Now Villiers and the Spanish alliance he desires are the targets for attacks by the House."

At the Parliamentary session of November 1621, petitions for religious liberty were sent to King James. Debates also centered on the rights of free speech in the House. One noted member, after frank and vigorous exposure of the nation's grievances, was tried by the Privy Council and sent to prison.

Word of this wicked act made Roger uneasy about his old friend. Two days after Christmas he went to see him. As he neared the house, he was amazed to see a crowd about it. The door was open and on the threshold stood Coke's body servant, wringing his hands.

Dashing up the steps, the boy cried out, "What has happened?"

"Oh, sir," wailed the servant, "the master! The King's men have taken him to the Tower. They have broke in his study, searched out his papers, and made off with whatever they wished."

In vain Roger tried to discover the reason for the assault. Finding the servant knew nothing, he ran to Westminster as fast as his legs could carry him. Hardly had he stepped into the great hall when he had the luck to meet young Edward Whalley, John Hampden's cousin.

Briefly Whalley reported the incident. Sir Edward and the great legal scholar, John Selden, had both made hot protests against the arrest of the man flung into jail for his speech on grievances. As the two came out of St. Stephen's Chapel where the House sat, they were surrounded by the King's guard and whisked off to the Tower.

"It is an outrage," concluded Whalley, "and my cousin is much aroused. But do not look so frightened, Mr. Williams. No one believes harm will come to the brave old gentleman."

Praying for his safety, Roger went every day to Coke's house for news. At last at Westminster he saw John Hampden. Then he learned that Sir Edward had been brought before the Privy Council for questioning and was expected home immediately afterwards. With Hampden and several others, Roger waited anxiously in Sir Edward's drawing room.

Finally his coach rattled up before the door. As Coke entered the room and saw his friends gathered to greet him, tears sprang to his eyes. He looked pale and worn. In a tired voice he announced the Privy Council's sentence.

"On pain of arrest, I may not lift my voice again during this session of Parliament. I am banished to my house at Stoke."

Cries of mingled relief and anger filled the room. After a time Sir Edward said calmly, "I shall continue my work on the Common Law. But only death can keep me from returning to the battle later."

When Roger shyly came to bid his patron good-by, he was told that he was expected down at Stoke the moment school vacation came. "Work well, my lad!" said Sir Edward with a friendly pressure of the hand.

That was all the schoolboy could do to prove his loyalty. Whenever he writhed in impatient longing to be at work for England's freedom, he remembered his friend's command. Such high marks did he win that a year later he received a most astounding reward.

3

IT was at Stoke that he was told. He was going to be sent to
Cambridge. As a Steward of the University, Sir Edward Coke
had secured for his promising protégé a scholarship at Pembroke College.

Cambridge! A chance to prepare for a profession! Roger
thought first of his father and wished he had lived to know about
such a wondrous turn of fortune. His death the previous year
had involved Mrs. Williams in new business responsibilities and
neither she nor his brothers paid any heed to the schoolboy in the

family. Roger looked at Sir Edward with passionate gratitude.

"You must discover your own chief interest, my boy," said Coke. "Yet I hope you will lean toward the law. Already you have a grounding in it."

At this the radiance in Roger's face dimmed a little. Those days in the Star Chamber had convinced him that, until reforms went through, the lawyer's work led nowhere. He managed to murmur that he could do no less for his generous friend than consider such a course.

Travel from London to Cambridge was monopolized by a man named Hobson who ran a hackney coach. At the University he kept an inn and livery stable. For the latter enterprise he laid down a rule that no customer could pick out a favorite nag, but had to take the first horse he saw. From this arose the humorous expression "Hobson's choice," meaning no choice at all, which is used this very day.

On the morning of his departure Roger found the coach at Charing Cross and three passengers waiting to embark. One, old and solemn, was obviously a don. Exchanging quips with the driver were two elegantly dressed young fellows. Huge plumed hats, embroidered velvet capes, rose-colored rosettes on high-heeled boots, proclaimed the height of fashion.

Innocently eager to share his own excitement, Roger stepped toward them. "Prithee, sirs, are ye, perchance, men of Pembroke College?"

Two pairs of surprised eyes traveled up and down his cheap costume of sober black. Shoulders shrugged. Brows lifted. Titters were exchanged. Then, turning their backs upon the intruder, the youths began a furious chatter about the birthday masque seen the previous night at some great London ball. At Hobson's signal, they scrambled into the coach and plumped down in the best places.

Cheeks burning, Roger sank into a seat beside the don. "Sons of great lords!" thought he. Stabbed by a sharp loneliness, he stared out of the window. Doubtless at the University many young bloods felt only scorn for Puritans. Suddenly a glimpse of Westminster Abbey's spire changed his mood. All the men of Parliament whom he admired—Sir John Eliot, John Hampden, John Selden, Sir Edward—would also meet haughty stares from these youths who prized only money and fashion. He grinned to think what glorious company he was in.

Arrival at Pembroke College brought an unexpected boon which raised his spirits. High marks in his entrance examinations had won for him a second scholarship, making him feel quite rich. He was lucky also in the roommates who shared his small cell. They were decent fellows with gentle manners. Happily he took up his stiff schedule of work.

One of the dons, Mr. Sandys, seemed delighted to discover Roger's interest in public affairs. Together they bemoaned the most recent bid for that alliance with Spain which was ruining England's prestige among all the Protestant countries. Villiers, now Duke of Buckingham, was actually in Madrid with Prince Charles, to arrange the latter's marriage to the Infanta. At home the political power of the Episcopal bishops, with their seats in the House of Lords and their high places at Court, threatened religious freedom as never before.

"Episcopalianism," lamented Sandys, "insists on outer ceremonies, on using the Prayer Book instead of the Bible, and permits not the slightest difference of opinion on doctrine. It goes hard with Puritans who wish simplicity, study of the Bible, and their own beliefs to prevail."

Roger looked thoughtful. "I am a Puritan. But my studies—above all, Hebrew—make me wonder if there should not be room for many beliefs. Puritans can be unchristian, too."

He laughed a little, thinking of an incident in the Pembroke quad. One evening he had been strolling there, enjoying the beauty of the moonlight, when three upperclassmen in Puritan dress passed by. One of them growled at him, "Moonlight addles the pate." Another sniffed, " 'Tis late for mooning."

At that instant Old Tom, the great bell of Christ's College, began its booming. One hundred and one deep-throated strokes it made, and on the last the college gates were closed for the night. The group of students paused to count the strokes. Presently the count reached ninety. Then ninety-eight.

A terrific racket at the gate blurred Old Tom's voice. Pell-mell, a half dozen figures rushed into the court with roars of laughter and loud curses at the porter. With plumed hat at a rakish angle, the leader staggered against one of the black figures in the silent trio.

" 'Ods Blood, that was close!" he shouted.

"Aye," panted the second fugitive. "One more tankard and we'd be out sleeping on the fens."

Savagely the older man pushed away the youth who had fallen against him. "Oh, learned master of the drunken arts, stand up!" he jeered.

"Hah, old Puritan!" yelled another reveler. "Go preserve thy soul in vinegar!"

Suddenly spying Roger, all six seized hands and spun around him singing, "Hey, nonny, nonny!" With folded arms he stood laughing at them and, when one boy fell flat upon his face, stooped and helped him up.

"What! Wouldst aid a sinner?" asked the boy. "No Puritan, you!"

The comment startled Roger. Yet he met men of that faith who thought it sin to laugh at folly or enjoy a comedy or even sing a madrigal. Often he wondered whether the charm of the Cambridge scene was wholly lost to such students. With its fortress-like towers, its green courts and avenues of trees, its river Cam curving a loving arm about its body, the University was a place of peace and beauty.

Sometimes, however, he feared it was too peaceful. After a year's work he found that original thinking on a student's part was not encouraged by the faculty. What the doctors praised was facility in Latin and Greek. The great truths offered by the ancients were seldom discussed. When Roger tried to get some light on his many speculations, he was rebuffed.

Often on warm afternoons he lay stretched on the grass by the Cam, pondering the problems of religion. How could a man best find his way to the Divine? Why was nothing said about a man's relation to his fellows by teachers and preachers? They didn't care half so much about liberty as did the political warriors who frequented Coke's house.

During his Easter vacation in 1625 when Roger went down to Stoke, Sir Edward greeted him with news. Marriage with the Infanta was off for good and the Duke of Buckingham had come back from Madrid with Prince Charles. Since both of them had

turned violently against Spain, they were taken into favor by the populace.

One morning as Roger helped his patron copy manuscript, the peace of the library was suddenly shattered. Horsemen came pounding up the drive amid a hullabaloo of cries and shouts. Still in his tasseled nightcap, Sir Edward hurried with Roger to the terrace. A crowd of excited villagers had run to the manor house behind the horsemen. Everyone was shouting and waving hats and caps. Leaping from the saddles, the messengers bounded up the steps.

But Sir Edward had already caught the meaning of the shouts. Catching Roger's wrist convulsively, he cried, "God in Heaven! King James is dead!"

All day Stoke hummed with excitement. Neighbors dropped in and a number of gentlemen rushed down from London. Everyone wondered what the sudden change would mean to England. Gleeful villagers and farmers, crying "Long live good King Charles!", evidently hoped for a better future. But Sir Edward's friends had other things to say. Some of their whispered comments left Roger thunderstruck.

When he returned to Cambridge he found the place astir. Flags at half-mast were hung out everywhere. Crowds in the village were matched by others about each college gate. Lads shouted their heads off for the uncrowned King. Masters huddled in knots of solemn talk.

At dinner next day Roger heard again the report that had so appalled him at Stoke. Two of the older students were talking in low tones, but fragments of their conversation reached him. "How can they be sure it was the Duke?" . . . "The King's physi-

cian . . ." "Too sudden was the death . . ." "Who else had ac-
cess . . ."

After chapel in the evening Roger was hailed by Mr. Sandys.
Marching the youth to the dons' study and planting him by the
fire, he said in a hushed, breathless voice, "Mr. Williams, I must
know . . . what do men of public trust, such as are known to
you, say of this rumor? Can it be true that the death of King
James was . . . unnatural?"

Roger reported all he knew. On the morning of the King's
death his physician found on the bedside table a bottle of strong
medicine which he had not prescribed. The King had been ill,
but not near death. Shocked out of all discretion, the physician
had accused the Duke of Buckingham of hastening his master's
end. Villiers was one of the few who could enter the royal bed-
chamber at any time. Moreover, the Duke's loyalty had shifted
from King to Prince, and he was most eager to see Charles on the
throne. At Stoke, Sir John Eliot had told Coke the case was sufficiently suspicious to come before Parliament.

Sandys listened intently. "What villainy!" he muttered. "And
what retribution! A king who wished to rule alone destroyed
by the favorite he had raised up." Meeting Roger's grave assent,
the tutor asked, "And now is it true that Buckingham chooses
Princess Henriette of France as the royal bride?"

There was no rumor about that. It was a fact. The alliance was
announced at Cambridge even before the memorial service was
held for James First. On that day of formal mourning, when
all the students were lined up to march to St. Mary's Church,
Roger heard nothing but comments about the romance. "What
will the Queen be like, think you?" whispered a youth behind

him. "A rare beauty certainly, and with a French grace!" was the answer. "Be this love or politics?" asked another lad. The man beside Roger turned around, grinning. "Fie, for shame! If the King love her not in France, he will love her in England!"

For weeks on end the King's wedding was the popular topic at the University. Before it had lost its savor, the grimmest of events swept light-heartedness away. Roger chanced to be first to hear of the stalking terror. To arrange for a trip to London to see his mother, he had gone to Hobson's livery stable and saw Hobson just driving up in his hackney coach.

At Roger's question, the old man burst out, "Nay, nay, sir, ye cannot go to London now. I'm just back from there and death walks the streets. Funeral processions crowd every lane. Already houses are barred and shops closed. Everyone flees the city and I brought out more than the coach could well hold. God save us, what a fearful time!"

"But what? Why?" cried the youth.

One muttered word explained. "The plague, sir! The plague!"

Once the news spread through Cambridge the place was in a turmoil of departures. Doctors, dons, and students left the place almost empty. A letter from Sir Edward came to Roger begging him to hurry to Stoke. But he wrote a grateful refusal. He promised to be careful. But he was not afraid and needed every moment to prepare for taking his degree.

Indeed, in the quiet of the deserted place he made swift progress. Hardly did he set foot outside the quad. He wrote his mother that he ate no fresh fruit. "Nought is safe to eat in this place save eggs, custards, and apple pies," he reported. From the outside world filtered reports that Parliament was sitting at Oxford. Only poor folk remained in London. But slowly the news grew better. The plague receded. Students drifted back and by autumn the halls were almost filled again.

Before Roger took his degree in January 1626, he had a difficult task to perform. For the first time he went to Stoke with a heavy heart and a troubled conscience. Within the hour of his arrival he blurted out what he had come to say.

"Sir Edward, I am at a cross-roads. Shortly I take my degree and the future is upon me. God knows it is hard to tell you—I had hoped—I know you wish me to study law, Sir Edward. But that I cannot do. It seems to be God's will. . . . I have thought much. Sir, I mean to become a minister."

"A minister!" Sir Edward's shout rattled the porcelain vase on the mantel shelf. "By the Holy Rood, this is folly!"

He strode to the fireplace. Then he whirled about. "Hast thought what a Puritan minister meets in England today? King Charles hath made Archbishop Laud his most trusted counselor. His Majesty supports the plan to crush all religious groups outside the Church of England. In time every Puritan preacher will be silenced. The pillory, the prison, or exile will await you. Hundreds of ministers have fled with families and followers to Holland. Some have even found rough refuge on the coast of Massachusetts."

Without a glance at the pale, suffering face of the young man in the corner, Coke began to pace up and down. "I had thought, Mr. Williams, you would follow me into the law. Gladly would I pay for your instruction at the Inns of Court. Hath law no drag upon your wishes?"

Now at last his blue eyes stared straight at the drawn face of his companion. Bravely Roger answered, "No, Sir Edward. Mind and soul both act in one toward theology. I am beckoned to the ministry irresistibly—beyond reason mayhap."

"Aye, beyond reason!" With a loud snort Sir Edward paced six steps and came back to shout, "If you be imprisoned or exiled, Mr. Williams, what end will you serve by being a minister?"

At this Roger stood up, tall and gracefully poised before his angry friend. In a tone firm for all its gentleness he said, "I cannot name the end in a precise manner, sir. I understand that you likely feel ill repaid for your great generosity toward me. But now, at least, I can shift for myself in taking up studies for the ministry. That is what I came to say."

There was a long pause. Sir Edward shook his head, sighed, and at last faintly smiled. "Ah, well, boy, think not I am like His Majesty who rules without consent of his subjects. Here's my hand on it. Your scholarship will continue. You have worked hard for it—God bless you!"

Roger seized the wrinkled hand and pressed it in both his own. His heart bounded with pride in his patron. Here was a man who had proved his belief in liberty of conscience.

As for the dangers to dissenting ministers which Sir Edward had listed, they drew close to Cambridge within a few months. In May 1626 the Chancellor died. Immediately King Charles asked the University to elect in his place the Duke of Buckingham. Everyone knew that, under the Duke, Archbishop Laud would begin to lay down the law to the theologians. Storms of protest arose against the King's candidate. Students and faculty divided into camps and excitement ran high.

On election day Roger pushed his way through the crowds outside the Senate Hall. Surely, he said to himself, a great university will not shame itself by choosing this royal minion! All hope died with the opening of the Senate doors. The Duke had won by three votes.

Heavy on England's neck lay the hand of arbitrary power. Buckingham's fiercest opponents in Parliament, John Hampden and Sir John Eliot, had been whisked off to prison. Now the King was setting his people against the very war they had long desired. At last they had a chance to defend a group of Protestants against their foes. The French Protestants were besieged in Normandy by their own King Louis and his Cardinal. Lately England's foreign policy had brought it into conflict with France and preparations had begun for rescuing the brave people fighting for life and liberty in Normandy. But British shouts of joy were soon stilled by King Charles. By forcing loans, gifts, and revenues to pay for the war without consent of Parliament, the King aroused stubborn resistance from the nation.

Roger, who followed events with breathless concern, found the apathy at Cambridge incredible. With every sign of enthusiasm Buckingham was welcomed into office. On the March day of his induction as Chancellor in 1627 bells pealed out in all the chapel towers. Post riders galloped through the town with a great tooting of horns. Banquets and dinners were arranged in the Duke's honor and to greet him all the students marched in a grand procession to St. Mary's Church.

Young Williams, Bachelor of Arts, took every step in protest. He longed to stop his ears to the sudden shout, "There he is! Long live the Duke of Buckingham!"

Near the entrance of St. Mary's the new Chancellor stood beside the President of Cambridge. With one jeweled hand pushing back his short coat of emerald velvet, the dazzling figure seemed far prouder than when Roger had first seen him as Lord Villiers in the Star Chamber.

Was the favorite deceived by a crowd of boys crying, "Long live our Chancellor!"? Did he imagine the nation was with him? Roger took comfort in a report from his patron that from every corner of England had come messages of encouragement to Parliament. Every item in the Petition of Rights recently drawn up was known to farmers and villagers throughout the realm.

On a visit to London Roger had had a chance to study that Petition. It rehearsed the laws framed to protect the people's rights. Statutes made it illegal to impose taxes without consent of Parliament; to punish anyone without due process of law; to billet soldiers on the people. Yet all these acts and more had been committed since Charles First was crowned.

By a vague rejoinder His Majesty made it plain he had no intention of signing the Petition. 1628 began with storm clouds thick over Westminster. Sir John Eliot, released from prison in a state of broken health, was back in the fight. It was he who brought the storm pelting down. Listing the mistakes and offenses of the Duke of Buckingham, Sir John declared reform must begin with his removal.

But no criticism of the King's ministers could be allowed! So said the Speaker of the House. In the death-like hush, every member listened to the knell of free speech. "The kingdom is lost!" cried a voice like the sound of doom. Groans and sobs were heard along the benches.

Suddenly Sir Edward Coke's voice roared out. He proposed

that the Remonstrance ready for submission to the King include a statement that Parliament had no quarrel with His Majesty, but only with that source of all evil, Buckingham. Unanimous vote carried the motion.

When Coke reported the scene to Roger, he said, "We must fight on. But King Charles doth refuse to learn that absolute royal power is a thing of bygone days."

London seethed with reports of Laud's persecution of Puritan ministers. The Archbishop was transforming simple services into pageants of ritual. Robes for the minister, candles for the altar, prescribed sermons ordered from above! Recently a letter had been sent to every bishop in England with orders to urge ministers of the diocese to preach on the divine right and absolute power of the monarch. Obedient bishops promptly received promotions or other favors.

Parliament heard a strong protest against this outrage to religion. A new member reported the facts and boldly said that the Church was fast becoming a mere tool of the Crown. The fearless Puritan who spoke was known only to a few. At Cambridge Roger could find out nothing about him. But he meant to learn more of this protester named Oliver Cromwell.

Would that some such voice could be heard from the University Senate! The Archbishop, with the new Chancellor's approval, was beginning to dictate Cambridge policy. He had ruled that every course in preparation for the ministry must meet with his approval. That meant that even the most timid effort of independent thinking would be snuffed out.

Roger discussed the situation with Mr. Sandys over a cup of tea in the don's study. "You see, sir, after I take my Master's degree this summer, I must choose. Either I continue here in the studies required for a degree in theology—a matter of several years' more work—or I leave the place for good."

"But I thought you had decided the matter and meant to stay." The tutor raised surprised eyes to the anxious face turned toward him.

"Aye, Mr. Sandys. But this ruling changes all. Courses laid out by Archbishop Laud are only good for puppets."

Sandys groaned. "I agree. What is your alternative, Mr. Williams?"

Briefly the youth sketched it for his adviser. As a Master of Arts, he could take special coaching and go before a bishop for examination. If qualified, he could take Holy Orders and then find a living in some small country parish.

"To rot there?" barked the tutor harshly.

"Nay, sir, to discover what best service I may find in life."

His listener was silent. Softly the logs hissed and crackled on the hearth. Quietly then, as had often happened before, Roger felt the atmosphere lift about him, was aware of a presence in his heart that was not himself. Time seemed to stop. And when he took leave of his host, he knew that his decision had been made.

4

HURRY, Mr. Williams! We shall be late!"

With a start Roger looked up over the pile of books on his study table at his roommate who had just come in.

Meeting that puzzled glance, the speaker said, "Have you forgotten the undergraduate disputation we must attend this afternoon? The don said none will be excused."

Springing up and snatching his cap, Roger said impatiently, "I had forgotten and I begrudge the time. I need every moment to prepare my Latin discourses for graduation."

Nevertheless, on a distant day he was glad he had not missed

the debate that afternoon. The whole occasion was made inter-
esting by one of the underclassmen from Christ's College. Not
only was his Latin speech brilliant but his appearance was strik-
ing. Tall and slender, the youth had beautiful fair curls falling
over his fine linen collar and a skin of delicate tint. In contrast
were the lofty brow and noble expression of great, dark eyes.

At the end of the disputation Roger inquired about the student
of another Christ's College man. "Well, the fellow is said to be
something of a poet," was the amused answer. "His name is John
Milton, but for his dainty disapprovals and his fair complexion
he is dubbed 'The Lady.'"

"'Tis a lady out of Mr. Shakespeare's plays then," said Roger
warmly. "His was a rare disputation."

Roger's own Latin speeches on Commencement Day gave him
no sense of triumph. He could not put his heart into them. Yet
he felt a youthful excitement over the great ceremony at St. Mary's
Church and over the superb scholarship shown by a few gradu-
ates. It was fun, also, to watch the visitors crowding the town. The
fine parade of silks and satins splashed color over the throng of
black-gowned figures. Food and wine were snatched on the run
from one audience room to another. But in the evening after the
program was over feasts were held in all the college halls.

Wearied by the long day, the new Master of Arts was strolling
into Pembroke quad when the sight of a familiar figure quickened
his step. "Sir Edward!" he cried delightedly.

Coke left the gentleman beside him and held out his hand.
"You did well, Mr. Williams," he said cordially. "And now what,
my friend? Do you continue your studies for the theological
degree?"

Roger told him he was only staying through the summer to be coached privately and would then try to take Holy Orders. Coke shrugged, stroked his white beard, and muttered that it might be better so.

As usual the old man plunged at once into politics. Buckingham, he reported, was gathering a good fleet and a body of soldiers to relieve the French siege of the Protestants at La Rochelle. John Hampden was now on a committee to deal with church reform.

"Tell me, Sir Edward," asked Roger eagerly, "who is the new antagonist of the Established Church, Mr. Oliver Cromwell?"

Coke snorted. "That man, whose clothes were made by a country bumpkin, who hath neither manners nor address, is claimed by John Hampden as cousin. Hampden sees great promise in the fellow."

A cousin of the great John Hampden! In that case, thought Roger, he might some day meet Oliver Cromwell face to face.

Asked about his recently published work on Common Law, Sir Edward said, "I am beginning the second book, my friend. I grow too old for the hot fight of Parliament." He sighed, then leaned to whisper in his companion's ear. "Yet I should like to stay until we have deposed the Duke forever."

Less than two months later these words sprang to Roger's memory. Still at work in the Cambridge libraries, he was finishing supper at a small village inn one August evening. All at once the sleepy summer quiet was slashed by the rapid clap of hoof beats. Rushing to the window, diners saw a horseman gallop by at a furious pace.

"Only a messenger speeds so!" murmured Roger to the innkeeper. "There must be news!" Slapping down payment for his meal, he dashed out.

Instinct directed him to the President's house. There, indeed, at the gate stood the sweating horse. In a moment a servant, with eyes bulging with excitement, came to lead the beast away.

The sight of Roger uncorked the news. "Oh, sir, Buckingham is slain! A madman hath stabbed the great Duke. He is no more."

Before an hour was up the University knew the startling details. Just at the moment of setting forth with his fleet for France, Buckingham had been murdered. A fanatic soldier named John Felton, without the slightest warning, had plunged a dagger into the heart of the King's favorite.

As the news traveled throughout England, the sensation was tremendous. Most of the nation rejoiced. Young bloods from universities and towns openly toasted John Felton. In London the assassin was cheered on his way to the Tower. King Charles, of course, was inconsolable and all the Court went into mourning.

But what political effect would the Duke's death have? That was what Roger longed to know. Not until he reached London in late autumn could he get a hint. It came from an old friend of his, a bookseller near St. Paul's Churchyard, who had sold him the first book he'd ever bought—Sir Walter Raleigh's *History of the World,* written while the great seaman languished in the Tower. The bookseller was a rare political gossip and had much to tell his young friend.

"Riddance of the mighty Duke has changed little thus far, alas! The Council sit in the palm of the King's hand and pinch money from everyone like robbers."

Of Archbishop Laud, now Bishop of London and member of

the Council, the bookseller said, "That little red-faced man is never idle. For breakfast he eats a Puritan. For dinner he licks the King's boots and for supper serves the Council ideas for beating the House of Commons to its knees."

Sparing a laugh for this picture, Roger asked hurriedly about the members of Parliament whom he knew best. He learned that each one was safe and free. But disaster had befallen two wealthy patriots from Essex County. Because they had refused a penny to the huge loans demanded by Charles without Parliament's consent, both had been imprisoned. When release came it was too late for the elder man, Sir Francis Barrington, who died from hardships suffered. The other, his son-in-law, however, was re-elected to Parliament.

"There's a brave soul!" cried the bookseller. "Hats off to Sir William Masham!"

"Sir William Masham!" echoed Roger in amazement. "But a week ago I saw that gentleman. He invites me to be chaplain of Otes, the parish in Essex where he hath his estate. I knew not of his sufferings and sorrow."

Hearing from the shrewd bookseller that Sir William was the finest type of Puritan patriot, Roger left the Churchyard feeling the die was cast. As soon as he had obtained Holy Orders, he would accept the post at Otes.

Since he was staying in London over Sunday, Roger asked his mother to go with him to the service at St. Sepulchre. But she shook her head with an angry look.

"A Mr. Peters, one of your Puritan ministers, doth preach there now, to great crowds they say, but not to me!"

Roger understood why the church was packed when he heard

the fearless eloquence of the sermon. But later he was sorry he
had lingered to meet the minister. Out of the pulpit Peters had
a domineering manner and suggested not a servant of the Lord
but a merchant bent on success.

Early in January the Cambridge Master of Arts was ordained.
A few weeks later he was comfortably settled in the Essex parish.
The family welcoming him at the manor house consisted of Sir
William and Lady Elizabeth Masham and the latter's seventeen-
year-old daughter by a former marriage. Her name was Judith
Althem, but everybody called her "Jug."

The chaplain's duties were far from hard. He had to preach in
the parish church, visit the sick, and read the Bible lesson to the
family. Plenty of time was left to knit together the strands of his
thinking about religion and politics and his own future.

One fine February afternoon a servant knocked at the door
of Roger's room. Was Mr. Williams willing to put aside his books
and drive with Lady Elizabeth to see her mother at Hatfield
Priory?

The answer was a delighted yes. Roger had already met Lady
Joan Barrington, a woman of great force, widow of the patriot
who had died as a result of his imprisonment. Her estate at
Hatfield was near by. These people were typical of the important
and wealthy Puritan families in that part of England and were
connected with all of them by blood, marriage, or friendship.

Lady Elizabeth, waiting on the terrace, presented a perfect
model of simple ideals of dress. Her bodice and ample skirt were
of brown baize and the deep linen collar around the high-cut
neck was unadorned with lace.

As Roger helped her into the carriage, she said, "My mother's niece, Miss Jane Whalley, is at the Priory now. Mayhap you have heard of her brother—my cousin, Edward Whalley, who is in Parliament."

"I have met him often, Madam. Long ago at Stoke which he visited with Mr. John Hampden I saw him first. Doth his sister also follow public matters?"

"See for yourself," said Lady Elizabeth with a little laugh. "Is that what you require of young ladies, Mr. Williams?"

That made him blush and stammer. But he soon found that among Jane Whalley's many charms was a decided interest in politics. It was the air the whole family breathed. Lady Joan's son, Sir Robert Barrington, was a member of Parliament and sat with his brother-in-law, Sir William Masham, on committees.

"My son writes me," said Lady Joan to Roger, "that King Charles depends more than ever upon Archbishop Laud and brooks no criticism of his acts. Be on your guard, young man."

"Then," said Lady Elizabeth, "His Majesty must have marked for dislike our cousin, Oliver Cromwell. I hear, Mother, that Oliver's speeches are much talked of."

Lady Joan sniffed. "That young man doth seem such a sloven it goes hard with me to think him either wise or able."

"But not with me, dear aunt," protested Jane Whalley in a voice of such sweetness as to make Roger's heart quiver. "Oliver is a most eager Christian and very active. He would restore the Bible to all who may only use the Prayer Book now."

When the visitors rose from their tapestried chairs to take leave, Lady Joan offered a gracious hand to the chaplain and murmured that he must come and dine some day. Thanking her, he watched Jane's wild-rose face.

That evening and next day he thought of nothing but the slender, soft-spoken girl. How lovely she was! Had she liked him? When would he see her again? Finding that neither study nor writing a sermon could smother these insistent questions, he decided that a trip to London might distract him. Lady Masham loaned him a horse, bade him God-speed, and he was off.

London in 1629 was enough to shake a man even out of a dream of love. On his very first walk to Westminster, Roger saw at Charing Cross a sight which nearly made him swoon. There, surrounded by a crowd that cursed the guards about him, stood a man in the pillory. His face, of noble cast, was deathly white, and a bloody gash at the side of his head showed that one ear had been cut off.

A well-dressed man in the crowd said to Roger in a tense voice, "Behold a Puritan minister, a man of God! Sir, he refused to set up an altar with a cross and make bows and wear a gown when preaching! For this crime Archbishop Laud hath sentenced him to punishment."

Shuddering, Roger hurried on. Ah, if only he could speak with the tongues of angels against such evil! It must be possible for men to create a society free of persecution! Englishmen were not fanatics. What kept them from religious liberty? His step slowed. With passionate intensity he groped for the reason. It seemed as if that mutilated figure in the pillory pled with him to deal somehow with the horror which had overtaken an innocent Christian.

Suddenly he touched a key to the problem. Persecution always happened when churchmen had civil power. Bishops could order out guards and troops to arrest and punish ministers who did not conform. As the truth seeped into the depths of his understanding, elation swept away pain. Now he knew the principle for which he meant to work with all his soul. Government and religion must act apart. State and church must be separated.

In the glow of this discovery Roger entered Westminster Hall. It was the hour when the Parliamentary session ended and already several gentlemen were coming out of the chamber. From afar he recognized John Hampden, sterner and much less dreamy than he remembered him. The tall man with frail body and burning eyes was Sir John Eliot. And just behind them, walking with youthful stride, came Sir Edward Coke.

"Mr. Roger Williams—well met!" boomed the familiar voice.

Both the other men greeted the youth cordially, and promptly all three whisked him off to a small tavern where they meant to confer in a private room. There one by one the key men of England gathered. Oliver St. John and John Pym came in promptly and later John Selden, legal genius of the Commons.

Briefly Sir Edward sketched for his young friend the incident they were discussing. A fresh outrage had just been committed by the King. Without legal warrant of any sort, he had sent his guards to search the rooms of several members of Parliament for private notes and papers which might be used against them.

"The whole House must issue a remonstrance," asserted Pym. "I shall visit certain members this evening." Indomitable courage looked out of the speaker's eyes.

As the pudding was served talk turned on church reform. Into the subject thrust the harsh voice of a man who had just come to the table. Hearing the newcomer's name, Roger riveted his gaze upon him. At last an old wish had come true. It was he,

the bold critic of the Church, Oliver Cromwell!

Cromwell had a smoldering passion about him which set him apart from the keener, quicker men in the group. With swift recollection of what both Coke and Lady Joan Barrington had said, Roger observed that Cromwell's neck-band was awry and none too fresh. But he was sure that Jane Whalley was right about the man's character.

"I tell you, friends," Cromwell was rasping out, "I do assure you that true religion is being crushed to death. Mr. Hugh Peters now! Ye know the great preacher at St. Sepulchre. He hath had to flee to Holland. I say we are but sheep led by that wolf, Archbishop Laud."

Peters! How swiftly that eloquent voice had been stilled! At Roger's gasp of dismay Cromwell's heavy eyes held him a moment. But another new arrival was leaning over the chaplain's chair.

"Mr. Williams, I have heard of you from my mother as well as from my sister. 'Tis good fortune to find you here."

It was Sir Robert Barrington and the two fell into animated talk. At last Sir Robert asked the chaplain to carry a letter back to be delivered at Hatfield Priory. Ah, what a chance to see Miss Whalley soon again!

On the day after his return to Otes, the young man took the letter to Lady Joan. Over the closely written page she sent a smiling nod to the young man who sat blissfully beside Jane Whalley on the French sofa.

"My son speaks highly of you, Mr. Williams," said she. "He declares that you know more about politics than most members of the House. You must stay and dine with us today."

"Ah," laughed Jane delightedly, "you are blushing, sir. Come, cool your hot cheeks for a moment in the garden."

That stroll changed the world. On the stony path the girl slipped slightly and caught her companion's arm. He put his hand over her slim fingers and felt an answering pressure from them. At dinner they exchanged secret glances and at parting, tender smiles. Never had the youth imagined such joy. Another visit made him sure he loved this charming creature. The fourth time he saw her, when she and her aunt came to tea at Otes, he felt certain his love was returned.

Taking courage in both hands, he wrote Lady Joan Barrington to propose for the hand of her niece. He mentioned his assets—education, a small sum he would inherit from his mother, enthusiasm for work. But the great fact was his love for Jane. Surely that could not be denied!

Yet it was and firmly. Lady Joan had other notions for her charge than marriage with a penniless young nobody. In a rage at his impertinence she made her attitude very clear.

Roger read the missive with mounting fury. What worldliness for an old lady! How unchristian! Dipping his pen in ire, he told Lady Joan just what he thought. Not till he had sent the letter off did pride give way to grief. He had lost Jane forever. She would not, could not, defy her aunt. Nor did his mother offer any healing for his wound. In fact, she agreed with Lady Joan that such a union would be quite unsuitable.

Lady Elizabeth Masham tried in vain to comfort him. "You see, both your mother and mine think truly of the future, as women must. I myself am busy with the matter of a proper husband for my daughter Judith. A poor man should have a wife able to count the pence and help in all ways in the house. Love will come to you again—and with good sense under his wing. I know it, Mr. Williams."

It was unthinkable to him that he should ever love again. His only hope was to let his love, his sorrow, and his anger be transformed into work. For a week he scarcely left his room. From study and reflection grew a sermon which he preached one Sunday at the parish church. As he stood in the plain, unornamented pulpit, there was something of the young prophet in his look.

Simply he announced his theme. "A man of true religion doth not content himself with prayer and worship, but actively strives to bring love to bear on human matters. Of these the one that cries loudest today is need of religious freedom."

He did not thunder nor denounce. But behind every word burned the pain he had suffered in boyhood over the funeral pyre on Smithfield and recently over the sight of a Puritan minister in the pillory. No true follower of Christ, he said in a ringing tone, could persecute his fellow man, no matter what that man's faith might be. The glowing dark eyes, fixed afar, seemed unaware that the congregation sat tense with amazement. When the service ended, he slipped away and walked back to the manor house across the fields.

Behind him he left a breathless group of people. Never in their lives had they heard such commands voiced. Not persecute the heretics? Not frown on Catholics nor banish Jews? The preacher had made the deeds of Archbishop Laud appear ungodly and that was well. But liberty of conscience for each and all—ah, that was revolutionary!

An echo of the sensation he had made sounded in the greeting the Mashams gave their chaplain at dinner. It held a stifled amazement. Later they drew him into an alcove and laid their fears before him. Did he not know that the Archbishop had spies everywhere to report what Puritan preachers said? Sermons like that meant imprisonment or worse.

With a wry smile Sir William said, "One of our neighbors spoke of you after church as 'divinely mad.' You must be more careful, sir."

He faced them, resolute and sure. "Indeed, dear friends, I am grateful for your kind concern. But 'tis not you, Sir William, who set an example in caution."

True enough. Masham had just lived through a terrific scene at the House of Commons. Protest against the King's seizure of private papers was twice denied discussion by the Speaker, acting on direct orders from the Throne. But the assembly knew its very life was at stake. In a tumult of cries and shouts, one member held the Speaker in his chair while the question was moved by Sir John Eliot and read out to the end.

Suddenly came an ominous knocking at the door. "Open to the Usher of the Black Rod!" cried a voice outside. In vain. The door of the Commons room was locked and the key lay on the table.

When the knocking ceased, the vote was taken. Unanimously the protest passed and members rose to cheer. After the din subsided, the door was unlocked again and in the distance could be heard the tramp of marching feet.

" 'Tis the Captain of the Guard and his armed band sent to force the door!" So ran the whisper around the room.

Quietly, as if nothing unusual had occurred, John Pym stood

up and presented an item of finance. Every eye was on the doorway. Presently it framed the bulky figure of the Captain. He stared. All was peace and order, open to inspection. Bewildered, the officer marched his men away and left behind him smothered laughter.

A week later Roger was in London once more. An appointment with Sir Edward Coke took him to Westminster at high noon just as the King's ministers were leaving the palace. Sir Edward named each one, but called special attention to the Comptroller of the King's Household.

"That is Sir Henry Vane, the most liberal of the lot, but still an enemy of Parliament. It is said his son Harry has recently become a Puritan. To cure him his father sends him to travel in Italy. What folly!"

Coke admitted to his youthful friend that it was not safe these days to work for law or liberty. Next day proof of this rushed into Sir Edward's drawing room in the form of Sir Robert Barrington. "Sir John Eliot is taken!" he gasped. "He is accused of being a traitor to the Crown! Even now he is on his way to prison—and others also!"

Roger, who was present with a number of others, saw Coke clap his hand to his heart as if he had been stabbed. "This means his death!" groaned the old man. "Sir John cannot survive another period in prison."

Longing to do some small thing for the doomed patriot, Roger eagerly accepted Sir William Masham's invitation to visit Sir John at the Tower. The great gate was guarded by stout soldiers in red tunics trimmed with purple and fine lace. They admitted the visitors into the court. Near the spot where glorious Raleigh and many another had met his end, they entered a gloomy fortress built along the river. Narrow as a coffin was the stone stairway winding darkly upwards to a corridor. At last a guard unlocked the door of Sir John's room.

There he was, writing at a table. Before he sprang up in greeting, Roger saw the tragic shadow in his fine dark eyes. "Welcome!" he cried in a tone vibrant as ever. "You see, thanks to Mr. Hampden, I now have quills, ink, and paper, and I begin a book on civil government. The King may still my voice but not my words."

When Roger rode back to Otes, it was in a strange mood of triumph. Lady Elizabeth, disturbed by all the news, expressed surprise at the look on his face. It was almost elation.

"These are days of greatness for England," he explained. "Such courage as I have witnessed! The Archangels side with patriots."

Nor was he shaken in this view when word came that Parliament had been dissolved. That it was not to meet again for eleven years he could not foresee. Yet he knew the conflict would be long. His confidence lay in the spiritual forces behind progress. The ancient wisdom handed down in Hebrew, Greek, and Latin, and his own meditations taught him of the power on which men could draw. Few among the circle at Otes, accepting the young chaplain as a person with wit, learning, and a lively friendliness, had any inkling of this mystic strain in him.

About his personal future he was quite uncertain. But through a door suddenly opened that late summer he glimpsed an unimagined vista. It was too strange to be tempting. Yet even before the maple trees turned gold about the manor house, his feet were drawn to the threshold of vast change.

5

AMERICA! That was the favorite theme of conversation at Otes through the summer of 1629. Letters from a new settlement on the Massachusetts coast had at last come back. Plymouth, of course, was an old story—nine years old, to be exact. But only the year before, in 1628, the town of Salem had been founded by families directly connected with the Puritan gentry. The Mashams and their friends, eager to follow the fortunes of the Pilgrims, were shocked to learn the heavy toll of life that had been taken by cold, hunger, and disease. Survivors, however, bravely rejoiced in their freedom from the tyranny of bishop and King.

One afternoon a group of guests at the manor house were seated in the far-famed Italian garden. Several of them were sipping the new hot drink called coffee made from a special kind of berry sent from the West Indies.

Lady Elizabeth recommended stirring in sugar. "The beverage may come into general favor, I think," she remarked. " 'Tis a pity coffee trees cannot be grown so far north as Massachusetts."

"But our company will soon be selling furs and lumber and fish," retorted her husband. "Then King Charles will be glad enough that he granted us a charter."

Sir William referred to the organization of the Massachusetts Bay Company. Some of the wealthiest Puritans in England had founded it and had obtained a charter from the King the year before. Although merely a trading venture in name and promoted as a good investment, the Company was a means of getting a foothold in Virginia, as all North America was called, for those opposed to England's established church. The Company's first move was to found Salem under the leadership of John Endicott. Now another settlement was being launched.

One of the guests said it was strange the King had agreed to charter a company formed by his enemies. Whereupon a strong voice replied, "Nay, not so. For well nigh a hundred years England hath wished colonies in Virginia. His Majesty welcomes every new settlement. As for the Archbishop, he would gladly see all Puritans vanish across the sea."

The speaker was Oliver St. John, a rich and clever young lawyer, friend of Hampden and lately the favored suitor for Judith Althem's hand. The girl's happy look suggested willing co-operation with her mother's plan.

"Aye, ye have it right," Sir William replied to him. "If King Charles and the Council and the Archbishop did look deep into our purpose, it is clear they cared not a straw."

"And the new settlement we prepare will not be opposed?" Sir Robert Barrington, another investor in the Massachusetts Bay Company, searched the face of his brother-in-law. "Would I might attend the meeting at Sempringham this month. With the Earl of Lincoln to support the conference and the Bishop of Lincoln to protect the Puritans, much should be accomplished."

"Indeed"—Oliver St. John leaned forward—"the expedition is certain to be arranged then. I hear ships are already commissioned to take the new settlers across the sea." A sudden glow came into his face. "Without the sailors who have made the sea lanes ours, we could do nothing."

Every Englishman shared the same pride. True, no Drake or Raleigh was now alive to capture the imagination. But there were many skilled, fearless captains and seamen, and their stout, small ships carried English woolen goods around the seven seas and brought back tea and spices, teakwood, silks, tobacco and sugar cane. Holland was Britain's great rival in trade, more powerful than either France or Spain. That the Dutch had settled New Amsterdam, the great port on the tip of an island called Manhattoes, was most unwelcome to the British. Even the Puritans, with every reason to be grateful to Holland for sheltering victims of religious persecution, resented Dutch success in sea trade.

Seated near his employer, the young chaplain of Otes had been listening eagerly to all the talk. Meeting his eyes, St. John said to him, "Is it true, what I hear, Mr. Williams, that you have been asked to head a church in Massachusetts?"

For an instant Roger was silent and the color rushed to his cheeks. The very sound of those words took his breath. Massachusetts! Might God's Will intend him to become part of that vast, unknown land?

At last he said, "Aye, Mr. St. John, it is true that such an invitation has been received by me. I shall certainly go to the meeting up at Sempringham to see what befalls."

With a friendly look, Jug Althem murmured, "You would be missed here, Mr. Williams."

"Amen to that," echoed Sir William Masham. "But he would be safer there."

Even Sir Robert Barrington chimed in with a kindly word. He had never been influenced in his liking of Roger by his mother's quarrel. Lady Joan had been ill all summer and away from the Priory. Lately it was rumored that her ceaseless effort to find a husband for Jane Whalley had fixed itself on a Puritan minister. When Roger heard this, he had sunk back into a mood of despair. His only cure for it was to remember how men were risking life and fortune for their beliefs.

It was in a mood of tense expectation that Roger set off one August morning for Sempringham. It was a long ride north and he was glad to be joined on the way by the Rev. Thomas Hooker. He was a middle-aged minister of great prominence as lecturer, a man of liberal opinions and of a courage too stubborn to be crushed.

When Roger asked him if he were meeting the Archbishop's interference, Hooker said, "My enemies at Court have written Archbishop Laud that suspension from the pulpit would not serve to silence me. For I could still hold private classes. No, they declare I must leave the country."

"And do you so plan, Mr. Hooker?" asked Roger with eager sympathy.

"Aye, Mr. Williams. I think of going to Holland for a while. Already have I written that strong preacher, Mr. Hugh Peters, who fled there. Yet Massachusetts may see me later. I feel my way in darkness."

When the two reached Boston on the English Channel, they added to their cavalcade an even more noted Puritan. This was John Cotton, eloquent preacher at the beautiful church of St. Botolph in the Channel port. Roger had long wanted to meet

the influential and scholarly divine. Rev. Cotton was handsome
and suave, with elegant manners and a beautiful voice.

To be one of this trio elated Roger. Never before had he had
the opportunity of discussing religious matters frankly with men
equally versed in theology. At dinner they mapped out the Protestant groups. There were the High Churchmen under Laud.
These wished to make the English Church exactly like the Catholic Church except that it would be independent of the Pope and
controlled by King and Archbishop. Low Churchmen wanted
only a reformed Episcopal Church with a simple service and a
godly group of bishops and rectors without political ambition.
Distinct from both were the more radical heirs of the two great
Protestant leaders, Luther and Calvin. These would do away
with the Church of England and substitute one free of bishops,
deans, the Prayer Book, and the ritual. But the latter groups dif-
fered widely among themselves both in doctrine and practice.

It seemed to Roger that his companions were really followers
of Calvin. Yet they spoke as if they still felt themselves part of
the existing Church. He declared frankly that he could not understand a mild non-conformity of that sort. The English Church,
he said, had so lost the spirit of Christ as to be both corrupt and
cruel.

At this he felt John Cotton's veiled eyes regard him doubtfully. Thomas Hooker expressed sympathy with Roger's view,
but added gravely, "Such opinions are strong for these times, Mr.
Williams. Word has spread from your parish that you are divinely mad."

Roger felt a shock to hear this phrase repeated. Yet, much as
he longed to agree with men he so much admired, he had to

differ with them on the subject of using the Prayer Book. The argument left him weary of being always on the opposing side. And whenever his spirits fell, the sharp ache in his heart came back. Had the lovely Jane Whalley become his wife, he could have withstood opposition cheerfully.

The next few days drained his strength. The meeting at the mansion of the Earl of Lincoln proved exciting. All who attended it were educated gentlemen and the most distinguished amongst them was John Winthrop, middle-aged, well dressed, possessed of genial manners.

The conference was lifted to the plane of adventure by a decision of the leaders. They resolved to transfer the headquarters of the Massachusetts Bay Company to America and to go themselves in large numbers to settle near Salem. The Earl of Lincoln's sister and his steward, Thomas Dudley, were both on the list of voyagers. A fleet of merchant ships was to set off as soon as the families could get ready.

At dinner on the last day of the conference Roger found himself seated beside Thomas Dudley. This conservative of advanced years said, "What think you of the changes made at these meetings in the Company's government? Have we advanced too far in freedom?"

Mentally Roger reviewed the set-up. A governor, deputy-governor, and a number of assistants were to be elected every year by Company members. The Governor was to call a monthly business meeting and also preside at an assembly of all freemen four times a year. Laws enacted by the assembly were to be enforced by magistrates.

At last Roger replied slowly, "But, Mr. Dudley, what of all

the men who are not members of the Company—the many arti-
sans, servants, and laborers who go with you? They will not own
land and so will not be freemen. If only investors in the Company elect officers and only freemen vote on laws, the majority
of the people will have no word to say."

After a frosty look of amazement at this response, Thomas
Dudley turned away without another word.

Every such discussion brought closer the terrific reality of
America. When Roger returned to Otes it was in a state of complete exhaustion. Next day he became seriously ill. Much alarmed,
the Mashams sent for their physician and arranged to have the
patient nursed. In her concern, Lady Elizabeth wrote her mother
begging forgiveness for the young man who still suffered from
his unhappy love affair. Lady Joan Barrington replied that when
she returned to the Priory she would receive the young hot-head.

Soon Lady Elizabeth could assure her mother that Mr. Williams was making a double recovery. His strength was returning
and his heart also had begun to mend. The cure was due to Judith
Althem's friend and companion, Mary Barnard, who had come
to stay with her as a kind of lady-in-waiting. Pretty, quiet, intelligent, Mary was an unselfish girl. She went with Jug to see
the young chaplain every day and Roger found Mary deeply sympathetic. Often she lingered to talk with him after her friend
had left, and the acquaintance ripened swiftly.

One day when she came with a bowl of soup, Roger was dressed
and lying on a couch. Mary leaned over him to arrange a pillow
and her hand touched the waves of his thick, dark hair. With a
glance of startled happiness at Mary's blushing face, Roger seized
the small hand. Turning the captured fingers over, he suddenly

thought of what Lady Elizabeth had said to him about the qualities of a helpmate.

"Your hand is one to do many things well, Miss Barnard," he murmured, "yet it is as gentle as a dove's wing."

In that moment the note of romance was sounded. As autumn drew on, it became evident to everybody at Otes that Mary and Roger had fallen in love. Judith was delighted and so was her mother. This time even Mrs. Williams approved her son's betrothal to a sensible girl who had neither fancy ideas nor ambitious relatives. And so it was in December at a little chapel in High Laver, Essex, not far from the sea, that Mary Barnard and Roger Williams were married and began their adventurous career together.

Roger secured a small, independent parish in Essex. But he and Mary were always welcome guests of the Mashams. Indeed, Jug demanded much attention from her friend in those early months of 1630. For her wedding with Oliver St. John was to take place in April.

Even that event did not change the atmosphere of the manor house. It continued to be a center for patriots. Stoke was another gathering place.

When Roger went to see Sir Edward Coke, he found him up to his old practice of writing on his law treatise in the early morning and conferring with radical leaders most of the day. Since Parliament was not meeting, it was more than ever important for men to agree on means of resisting the arbitrary monarch. John Hampden was already determined to refuse payment of "ship money" demanded by the King to build a fleet. Roger gave their plans his enthusiastic praise. But his powerful friends made no pretense of agreement with his own ideas.

" 'Tis gunpowder you burn in your pulpit," accused Sir Edward Coke. "Your sermons explode in far places. It becomes plain that you wish to cut adrift altogether from the Church of England. A Separatist are you, Mr. Williams! How came this to be so?"

With eyes fixed affectionately upon the indignant face of his old friend, Roger wondered what he could say. Intense study, meditation, and prayer had made certain convictions come clear. Chief amongst them was that freedom begins in a man's own soul and works outward into religious and political life. To Roger, therefore, a national church, dictating what people should believe and substituting for the Bible itself certain selections and ready-made prayers, was a real obstacle to progress. Was there any hope of putting such ideas to his patron?

At last he said slowly, "Sir Edward, you and Mr. Hampden and Mr. Cromwell and others may reform the Church. Yet its aim would still be to command men's thoughts about God. Must not each soul strive to find its own way to the Spirit?"

Shaking his head, the old man remarked gruffly that Roger went too far. The same words were used one summer day by Sir William Masham. He had called the young minister to Otes for conference and faced him with a look of deep anxiety.

"Mr. Williams, I cannot support your views. To oppose Popish ways in the church is well. To restore to mortals the image of Christ, as you do better than any I have heard, is a great service. But when you speak of a church with no authority from King or bishop, sir, you go too far."

Roger smiled at him lovingly. "You cannot protect me in this stand, I know, Sir William. Yet I must so speak to my hearers. No man can be compelled to believe anything, can he, Sir William? I go neither with England's Church nor with the Scotch Presbyterians who wish one church for all. Christ's ardor for freedom must not be snuffed out."

Utterly puzzled, the great landowner of Otes said mournfully, "Alas, Mr. Williams, you court Archbishop Laud's persecution. Behind prison bars, what can you do for freedom of thinking?"

To this question there was just one answer. Clearer and clearer it sounded with each warning. One evening Roger found a note awaiting him. Tearing open the seal, he glanced at the page and then drew Mary to him.

"Read this, dear heart. We must face the issue now."

Dated from London and signed "A Friend," the message told Roger that he was a marked man. Archbishop Laud was taking steps to have him brought before the King's Council for trial.

"Never must this happen!" For an instant Mary clung to him wildly. Then she lifted her face and her eyes grew starry. "What we have so often spoken of, now we must do. I am ready, my husband. Like Ruth I can say, 'Whither thou goest, I will go.'"

Roger held her tight. He had a feeling of leaping with her into space. His voice trembled a little. "It seems the only course. To Massachusetts we go, dear one, and may God be with us!"

In the end they had to rush. Another secret message reported that a summons for trial was on its way to Roger. He bade warm farewells to the family at Otes and hurried up to London for a stealthy good-by to his mother. She gave him her blessing and advanced a considerable sum of money from his inheritance.

Sorrowfully he had to give up going to Stoke for a last glimpse of his patron. As fast as coach could carry them, he and Mary set out by way of Windsor to Bristol. All the long miles they feared they might be stopped by the King's men.

When at last, however, they stowed their goods on the ship *Lyon,* the anxious pair could breathe once more. First of all they made the acquaintance of their shipmates.

"They seem good folk," said Mary tolerantly.

"Aye, Mr. John Throckmorton, especially, seems a man of excellent parts," remarked her husband.

Leaving his wife to rest, Roger took a stroll into the town. Soon he returned and leaned over her with face glowing. "A good thing hath befallen me, Mary. I just now met young John Winthrop, son of the man I saw in Sempringham who led the second party to Massachusetts. He would talk with me for a time."

Joyously the two young men set out for a tavern. To offset the chilly winter fog, they ordered glasses of western metheglin. Then and there they founded a lifelong friendship. Roger learned that John Winthrop, Senior, had been elected Governor of the colony in the place of John Endicott. Most of Winthrop's expedition had moved south from Salem to a spot boasting a fine harbor. They called the new settlement Boston in honor of the English port. Young Winthrop intended to join his father shortly and said he was certain Rev. John Cotton would have to seek refuge in Massachusetts.

"Mr. Thomas Hooker, now in Holland, may go with him," reported Winthrop, "but Mr. Peters delays yet a while. As for you, Mr. Williams, they have been expecting you in Boston for some time." He raised his glass and smiled. "To your good fortune and may the Lord bless your going!"

It was December first on a clear afternoon when Mary and Roger stood on deck to watch the shores of England recede. With arms linked, they braced themselves against the wind in silence. It was done! They were off on the great adventure. Mary's eyes said to her husband, "With you I am not afraid."

Thrilled by the wonderful, warm current passing from each to the other, Roger said, "Truly I glory in our going."

Nevertheless, even as he spoke, a wild doubt tore at his mind. There, fading fast in the sun-drenched distance, was the land where freedom's mighty battle was preparing. To leave the field of struggle was exile indeed. Only one possibility held hope. Straining his eyes toward the vanishing coast, he murmured soundlessly, "Pray God I may still in some fashion serve the cause of liberty!"

6

SIXTY-SEVEN days after the *Lyon* left Bristol, its anchor splashed into the waters of Boston harbor. Some twenty passengers stood on deck, watching the rocky shore. They saw hills dark with mighty trees set back from the ice-filled tidal inlets. Above the shore stretched small clearings and on them stood wooden houses, which at that distance looked frail as toys.

Winding down the frozen path to the water's edge could be seen a file of people. Cloaks whipped out in the bitter February wind. Hats and kerchiefs were waved toward the ship. As the first boatload touched shore, the travelers were greeted with warm expressions of thanksgiving. Roger and Mary Williams shared a look of awe and triumph at actually feeling beneath their feet the soil of America. At once they were singled out for special welcome. Everyone seemed to know of Roger and to be over-joyed that he had come.

Standing a little apart from the others, flanked by a servant on each side and grasping a gold-headed staff, was Governor Winthrop. Each of the newcomers was presented to him and received a word of greeting. To Roger Williams he held out a cordial hand.

"As a measure of our gladness, Mr. Williams, that God hath brought you safe to our shores, we shall soon declare a holiday. Meanwhile, sir, I trust that in the house assigned you for the

75

time being you and Mrs. Williams will find comfort."

Comfort was a word much changed by a sea crossing. In the small log cabin, already crowded by the family who had built it, Roger and Mary were not comfortable by any standards they had known in Essex. But they were so glad to be out of the tossing ship with its stuffy smells and its stale food that it seemed luxury to have a clean bed and a warm supper of hominy and broiled fish before the great open fire.

During the meal the travelers learned something of the hardships suffered by the new settlers. A pestilence had carried off a great number of them. To clear the land, prepare fields for crops, and build cottages for winter had proved a mammoth task. Yet this spot was liked better than Salem. There were many good springs and the harbor was excellent.

Early next morning Mary and Roger set forth to look about. The wind had dropped and the sun was out. Already some housewives had hung up their washing. A few moments' walk brought the two to an open space which, although merely a rocky mud-patch, they rightly took to be the village common. Roger glanced around at the bare frozen spaces stretching in all directions up to the forest. It was his first glimpse of a pioneer settlement and its starkness amazed him.

"Truly, wife, is this Boston?" he asked.

Mary laughed gaily. "Nay, 'tis only the bud of the town which one day will bloom here. While you talked with the Governor last evening, I was told many things. There, within that fenced enclosure, is the public spring where all come to draw sweet water. In that house opposite lives Governor Winthrop."

Roger swept his hand about. "When each house must have a

garden plot and some stand in the fields it makes a scattered sort of town. What are they building on that bluff? Didst find that out?"

"I did," replied Mary triumphantly. "That is to be a fort with guns trained on the harbor." She broke off with a cry, "Look! An Indian!"

The first Indian the pair had ever seen! He was coming down a far hill from a patch of woods. In the morning sun every detail of his costume could be noted—headdress of feathers, deerskin shirt, and long fringed trousers, blanket slung about the shoulders, moccasins on the feet. There was something regal in the carriage of his head and of his body, borne along in smooth strides across the frozen snow.

Roger gazed at him in admiration. "I must study the Indian language," he murmured.

But first he had to study the situation in Boston. A few days after his arrival Roger was invited by Governor Winthrop to make a tour of the settlement. He was enjoying the Governor's comments when suddenly they passed a large log house with barred windows and heavily locked doors. Looking wistfully between the bars were the faces of two men.

"I saw this prison yesterday," said Roger gravely. "Prithee tell me, sir, what were the offenses of these persons?"

Winthrop's voice hardened. "They broke our laws for keeping the Sabbath. Not only came they not to church, but they did fish in the inlet. Mr. Dudley himself saw them returning with their catch."

Roger walked on in silence for a moment. Then he asked, "Who tried them for Sabbath breaking, Mr. Winthrop?"

"The magistrates, Mr. Williams," said the Governor with slight impatience. "Constables brought the offenders to the magistrates and they were fined straightway and committed to jail for six days."

An inner convulsion shook Roger. Could there be no fresh start for building a society in a new land? Here in this wilderness was the same confusion of church and state which disrupted England. Controlling his furious disappointment, he made himself turn to the handsome gentleman beside him and deliberately note the noble qualities which had made Winthrop a leader. After that he could speak quietly and without personal blame.

"Sir, would it not, however, be more reasonable that the Elders should condemn and punish church members who break the Sabbath? Surely the duty of magistrates is only concerned with civil matters."

The Governor of the Massachusetts Bay Company stared at the speaker. Could it be? Was that low voice daring to question the methods by which the Colony established righteousness?

Reading his thoughts, Roger said with a smile, "Mayhap one day when we sit by a fire and are not walking in the bitter cold, we might talk of the problems of true government. Today I merely seek the facts."

He went on seeking them for many days. When he supped with Thomas Dudley and others called Assistants to the Governor, he learned every detail of this Puritan government. The more he learned, the sadder he became.

Observing his melancholy, Mary said, "Husband, art thou unhappy here among these folk? Surely they are kindly and make us welcome."

With that he could always agree. It was their ideas he found hateful. Nor was it long before the Bay Company discovered the fact. Its officers presented the newcomer with the highest honor at their command. Williams was offered not only membership in the Boston church, but the post of chief Teacher. Then they summoned him to deliver his reply. The meeting was held in the unwarmed hut which served as the Lord's House.

Facing the ring of grave gentlemen, the young minister searched the stern faces. He knew they wished to make certain of the candidate's theology. But after he had thanked them warmly for the offer, he told them why he could not take the post of Teacher.

First of all, the church was still joined to the mother church in England. Why should families come thousands of miles over sea if not to separate from the corrupt, autocratic, political machine called the Church of England? "Friends, ye should repent in sackcloth and ashes for the sinful connection!" he cried.

In the second place, he had come to understand that when religious and civil matters were tangled one with the other, liberty departed from social life. It was not within the rightful power of magistrates, elected by the Assembly, a civil body, to enforce commandments concerning man's duty to God. The church could justly make rules and punish those who broke them. But officers of town and Colony must serve the whole people, not the small number of church members.

Dumbfounded, the Elders stared at their youthful accuser. It was a new sensation for these men, completely powerful in the Colony, revered by many, obeyed by all, to have their ideas opposed. After a stunned silence, one after another flung furious questions at the challenger.

"Would you have a town where men went unpunished for heresy and blasphemy, Mr. Williams?"

"Why dost think we came to these shores save but to establish a God-fearing settlement? Sabbath-breakers cannot be part of it."

Governor Winthrop gazed at Roger in sorrow. "Mr. Williams, reflect!" he cried. "To us hath been revealed the true way to serve God best. 'Twas for that we came here. Is it not our duty as officers of this Company to punish offenders against the Lord?"

Roger looked into the angry, tight-lipped faces. Behind the semicircle of men he watched pass the dark shadows of narrow and backward ideas. These, he thought, had no place in the new land.

"Friends," he said in a persuasive tone, "let us in amity stir deeper together the waters of truth. For example, let us speak of those two put into jail for fishing on the Sabbath. Had they been disturbers of the general peace, they were guilty. But no deed can be more quiet than to fish. Nay, sirs, the punishment imposed your will in religious matters upon those who have not agreed with the Sabbath-keeping rules. Therefore in this ye are no better than the tyrants in England from whom we all have fled."

Paying no heed to the angry mutters passing from one of his hearers to another, he went on, "Ye do wrong on the two counts I have set before you. I am sensible of the honor ye do me. But I can have nought to do with a church still joined to the Church of England, breaker of the Second Commandment. Nor can I be content with a town government where magistrates do interfere with men's private liberty of conscience. Not by such means can we make Massachusetts a state fit for free men."

Only one or two of the Elders seemed to be weighing these words. Most of them showed the outrage they felt to have their offer declined—and for such reasons. It was incredible! For hours the group harangued the man who dared defy them. Not till early dusk closed in about the meeting house did the stormy session break up.

As he walked back to the log cabin in the icy twilight, Roger felt a great warmth rise within him. That question which had torn his being on the deck of the *Lyon* was answered. Here in Massachusetts he had the opportunity for which he had prayed—to fight for the cause of human liberty.

From that time forward Roger Williams was the most talked-of man in New England. People coming down from Salem and up from the neighboring Colony of Plymouth wanted to meet him. He had defied the ruling powers! Everyone who approved of the leaders considered him an upstart. But liberal-minded folk and those who held no property and many who did not belong to the church hailed him as a prophet. It was stirring that some one man had the spirit to speak against the rules they all hated.

Typical of this group was the cobbler who was making Roger a pair of thick high boots for wear in the forest. When Roger came in for a fitting, the cobbler drew his stool close beside the customer and said in a low tone:

"Mr. Williams, the Company officers fear your ideas will spread about the Colony. It is whispered they wish to put you on a ship for England."

Roger stared aghast. "You mean—such a plan is afoot?"

Wiping his hands on his leather apron, the other shook his

head. "Nay, I doubt if they dare offend those men with money in the Company. I have heard that a certain Sir William Masham and Sir Robert Barrington are good friends of yours. I pray God, sir, you will stay with us here."

Touched by the man's concern, Roger thanked him and went away. Mary greeted his return with the news that Governor Winthrop had sent him a packet of books with a kind message. The young woman was greatly surprised at this courtesy. But not so Roger, even with the cobbler's story fresh in mind.

"Mr. Winthrop is a friend of mine, dear wife, and generous. He regards me as an enemy to his cherished beliefs, but wishes me well, I know."

Roger was very busy these days getting acquainted with New England. He took a trip up to Salem by boat and another down to Plymouth. With a guide he visited all the near-by Indian camps and presently went alone for a long trip of exploration. In a short time he had mastered many Indian phrases and the forms of address to the chiefs which politeness required. A very practical reason pushed him into this effort. In order to work out a source of income, he wanted to start a trading business with the natives. From every contact with them he came back to Mary in a mood of exhilaration.

"These men are heathen beings and know nought of Christ's mercy, yet they are close to their gods and treat me with great civility. Can you understand, dear wife, that I am happy amongst them?"

What Mary Williams understood best at the moment was that she and her husband were suspended in space. By refusing to join the church he had put them both outside the community. Without a home of her own she felt like a plant with roots in air. Although she helped the family where they were staying, there was no lasting satisfaction in that. March with its wild winds and rain came and went and still she had no idea what they were going to do.

Then on April twelfth a number of gentlemen came to the house asking for Mr. Williams. When Mary received them, they told her they were from Salem. She went to find her husband with a lively hope that at last a means of settling down was going to be offered. And she was right. The moment the strangers left, Roger climbed up the ladder-like stairway to the upper floor where he knew she was carding wool.

Paying no heed to the other women and the many children in the loft chamber, he hurried to her side. "Mary," he said in a low, eager tone, "the Elders have called me to Salem to assist Mr. Skelton, the chief Teacher in the church."

Her eyes filled with joy. "Then we shall live there and have a house!" Even as Roger nodded happily, however, her face clouded. "But, husband, what of this church? Is it so different from Boston? Shall you be happy there?"

"I can join the Salem congregation with a free heart. Mr. Skelton doth also believe, as I do, that the churches in this land must be cut off from the Church of England. Already I have two good friends in that church, Richard Waterman and the same John Throckmorton who sailed with us on the *Lyon*." After a moment's silent reflection, he added, "Doubtless there will be protests from the Massachusetts Bay Company. But go to Salem we shall, and at once."

In the middle of April they set forth. It was a beautiful trail they followed north to Salem. The woods were perfumed with arbutus and starred with bloodroot and harebells. Willows along the brooks waved delicate green feathers. Bird songs filled the air. It was happiness for the two young pilgrims to be alone together again, to talk and laugh and plan.

As they ate their luncheon of bread and cheese beside a brook, Mary laid her hand on her husband's arm. "There has not been much peace for us in Boston town. Mayhap in Salem we shall fare better."

Roger, looking straight ahead along the trail, replied slowly, "Yet let us remember that we follow Him who brought not peace but a sword."

In the next stormy months of adjustment to the New World, the words became a prophecy.

7

"TELL me, my husband, is Mr. Endicott as important in Salem as Mr. Winthrop is in Boston?"

Mary Williams put down the stocking she was mending and Roger, lifting his head from the papers on the rough-hewn table, looked at her with an obvious effort to drop his absorption and pay attention to her question. The two were sitting alone in the candle-lighted, one-room hut which had been loaned them on the edge of Salem. Tiny as it was, the cottage might have been Mary's wish come true. If only she were sure they were going to stay there! Uncertainty of this had prompted her remark.

"Nay, Mary, not so," said her husband at last. "When Mr. Winthrop arrived last year, he was at once elected in Mr. Endicott's place as Governor. When he moved to Boston, authority over the Colony went with him." After a pause he added slowly, "Neither Mr. Endicott nor the people of Salem will go against the Bay Company officers by keeping me here against opposition."

That was what she feared. Boston Elders and officials had never stopped protesting that the defiant critic of their church and government should be Salem's Teacher.

At first the protests had no effect. Mr. Skelton, the Salem pastor, wanted a powerful ally to fight for greater freedom both in his church and in the town government. But conservatives in the town thought disobedience to Company authority was dangerous.

They murmured that if it came to a downright command from Boston, the church had best let Mr. Williams go.

Roger got up from his rough wooden armchair and threw a log on the fire. Turning, he said abruptly, "I believe, Mary, that Plymouth is the place for us. It is more advanced in independency."

Plymouth was then not part of Massachusetts, but an entirely separate Colony. Its backers and charter had no connection with the Massachusetts Bay Company. Most of the original settlers had spent years of exile in Holland and had come directly from there to America.

As he made this suggestion, Roger looked at his wife with tender sympathy. Well he knew these uprootings were hard for her. As for him, he had the satisfaction of struggle for freedom. In addition, he was deep in the enterprise he had grown to love— that of working out friendly relations with the Indian tribes. He was studying their language as hard as he ever studied Greek or Hebrew. Even before he left Boston he had, with the help of older settlers in the back country, mapped out a general picture of the various tribes.

In all New England there were only a few thousand Indians. These were grouped into five main tribes: Pawtuckets, near Salem, north and west; Massachusetts, dwelling around Boston Bay; Pokanokets, near Plymouth; Pequots, in Connecticut; and, most powerful of all, Narragansetts, living west of Narragansett Bay. All these tribes were small in number but had lesser tribes dependent on them.

The first English settlers at Plymouth found the New England tribes friendly. A terrible pestilence which had swept away many braves had left them in a softened mood and unready for war. Massasoit, sachem of a tribe subordinate to the Pawtuckets, became the sincere friend and helper of the Pilgrims. Thanks to this favorable beginning, Roger was well received in the wigwams and tepees. His eagerness to learn the Indian tongue, his respect for tribal customs, and his liking for the dignified chiefs made it easy for him to do business with the traders. Already he had collected for export furs which the ship captains declared would bring good prices.

When Roger came back from his first long expedition to the Pawtucket camp, Mary received him with amused admiration. As he undid his pack of skins, she cried, "Who, seeing thee now, would guess how lately this trader stood in an Essex pulpit preaching learned sermons?"

The trader grinned affably. "The wilderness maketh a man practical."

Watching another packet unwrapped, the young woman exclaimed, "Do those pretty beads go to London for fine ladies to wear?"

"Nay." Roger held up a string. "Such is Indian money. Look close. See how the small shells are sewed on strips of cloth. This string is made of white shells and is wampum. Six small beads equal an English penny. Here is a string of black shells from the poquauhock fish. It takes but three of these to equal a penny. This better money is called suckauhock."

Mary laughed gaily. "Truly thou comest home a rich man. But what can your wife buy with these shell pennies so strangely named?"

Roger glanced from the strings displayed along his arm to her merry face. With passionate warmth he replied, "Ah, my sweet, we could buy land with these little shells—land for our home in this new world!" Then he sighed. "But we must wait a bit before I can save so many fathoms of wampum. These now I must sell again. They are much desired in the Colony to buy corn and furs and rush mats and bowls from the savages."

It was all the more necessary for Roger to succeed in his trading enterprise because he would take no salary for teaching at the Salem church. That was part of his principle that there should be no "hireling ministers" to hamper religion. Many payers of tithes in Salem felt a puzzled gratitude toward this curious man who relieved them from supporting him.

Mary and Roger Williams had not been long in Salem when the Massachusetts Assembly held a meeting in Boston. The laws passed then set the pattern of New England's future. They ruled that nobody in the Colony should have a vote who was not a member of some church within its limits. Inasmuch as only about a fourth of the settlers were church members, a powerful minority rule was thereby set up. Roger Williams was horrified to learn of the statute.

"This is facing back to the past!" he cried mournfully to Mr. Skelton. "The Colony is now a theocracy as in the days of old when the priest was King."

From that time on Roger turned his face toward Plymouth. Before the summer's end he and Mary settled there. The town, now eleven years old, was better organized than those in Massachusetts. The Governor, William Bradford, a man in his early middle age, had directed the Colony from the first. He received Roger and his wife graciously. Through his influence the magistrates assigned the newcomers a house and farm land.

Before snow fell the pair were well settled. Wood was piled in the shed. A cow was lowing in her stall. Onions, flour, and corn were stored on shelves near the fireplace, and Mary was happily feeding the hens that gave them precious eggs. Week by week they struggled against the cold and learned how to survive in fair comfort the bitter New England winter.

Often Mary wondered if her husband was content at Plymouth. She knew he approved the democracy of the church organization. For here the whole congregation met to conduct affairs and elect officers. The members, and not the clergy, held control. He was therefore happy when he was asked to assist the minister and to "prophesy" or speak on the gospels to the congregation.

In the spring of 1632 Roger set himself to learn farming. Almost every evening he went to some neighbor's house to get advice. Next day he was spading and planting, clearing out stones, putting into practice what he had been taught. He was so grateful for help, so boyishly pleased when he succeeded, so reverently interested in the mysteries of the growing process that the more experienced farmers delighted in coaching him.

It was a crucial year for Plymouth. For leaders in the Colony were proposing that the whole system of production and trade should be revised. For a decade the colonists had tried to live like early Christians. Before coming to America they had been inspired to do so by the lovable leader of their church in Holland. Land had been held in common and whatever produce was shipped to England was supposed to bring equal profits to all. But the system had not been a success. Energetic workers felt that in this new country a man ought to be able to get ahead for himself.

Two critics of the communal ideal came to find out Roger's opinion. One of these was Miles Standish, captain of the militia. "We ship but a thimbleful of corn and all too little lumber," he growled. "Salem will outstrip us in trade in the wink of a cat's eye."

The other visitor was the eminent Edward Winslow, one of the founders. He said thoughtfully, "It is of little use for my servant to raise good seed or to care for it, if I have to share it with reckless fools."

Roger's face was radiant. "Aye, friends, a man is himself first and a member of the Colony second. It is plain I cannot trade except on my own account. 'Tis best for each man of good health and wits to profit by his own work."

At the town meeting the new laws were voted. Individual effort was freed. And before many months had passed, it was plain that prosperity was going to increase.

That autumn after his grain was threshed and his turnips and cabbage stored away, Roger set out to visit Massasoit. By this time he could speak the language fluently. He could even make little jokes. As the Indians love to laugh, they enjoyed this visitor. He asked them much about their religion and, in turn, told them about Christ, Bringer of love and light. But he had no impulse to urge them to adopt Christianity. Any conception of what it meant was beyond their understanding, he felt.

This particular trip was a long one. Massasoit's village, called Sowams, was in the far southwest of the Massachusetts grant on a peninsula which jutted into Narragansett Bay. As soon as the traveler appeared, he was brought to the sachem's tepee. Made of logs and clay, it was heated by a wood fire, but as the hut had no chimney, it was full of smoke. Near the glowing coals women were drying fish and naked children were tumbling about on rush mats. For a moment the Englishman stood at the door trying to accustom his eyes to the darkness and his nose to the evil smells. Then he moved forward to greet the chief.

For the first time Massasoit seemed cold. With mere courtesy he received the gift of sugar his guest had brought. Presently Roger asked if something troubled the spirit of his host.

Something did. The chief had begun to doubt the English. Ship after ship brought more Englishmen, he complained. Ever more woods, the hunting grounds of the braves, would be chopped down for raising crops. Why did these strangers think they could seize great tracts of land? Forever it had belonged to the Redmen, given them by Keesuckouand and Nanspaushat, the Sun-god and the Moon-god. Englishmen called themselves righteous. But did they bring love and justice to Indians? No. They spoke as friends, yet their presence was to be feared.

Roger listened gravely. After a long silence he replied in a voice of warm friendliness. "I, too, great Sachem, have been troubled by these matters. Man is sinful and the justice of God comes slowly on earth. Englishmen should be sorry for their misdeeds and try to make them good. Yet they truly prize the friendship of the Indian and may grow worthy of it. Let us all have patience in overcoming evil. Speaking the truth, as we speak this day together, is the way of friendship."

Squatting in a ring about the sachem, other princes of the tribe listened intently. *"Wunnaumwaw ewo!"* murmured several voices, meaning, "He speaks true." One of the elder braves started a religious discussion by saying that since the English had clothes and guns and knowledge which the Indians did not have, their God must be more powerful than Indian gods. Roger replied that white men had struggled for many centuries to reach their present status and that the Indians could learn slowly all that the English knew. Before the council broke up and trading began, Massasoit made a little speech.

"English not all good. But this man our friend. We trust him."

After Roger's return home he worked every evening at a message which was the direct outcome of the trip to Sowams. When the pamphlet was finished, he took copies to the pastor and other influential people and sent one down to Governor Winthrop. Soon everybody in Plymouth was talking about the ideas Williams had put forth.

No settler, he declared, had a right to land except by direct payment to the Indian tribe that owned it. True, the English King had given the colonists a trading charter. But royal permission assured only the right to purchase land from the original owners. Anyone with a sense of justice knew that to steal land from Indians was no less wrong because they were heathen.

A bomb shell! Men who had agreed with Williams about the wickedness of the Church of England, men who had taught him farming, those who had praised his "prophecies" in church, now drew away in disapproval. He had touched their pocketbooks! Only a handful of Plymouth folk came to tell him he was right.

Governor Winthrop wrote the author of this pamphlet in a mood of great agitation. The King in Council had charged the settlers to buy land from the original owners. Therefore, if these opinions reached London, His Majesty might withdraw the charter altogether.

Roger replied that the pamphlet was written for Plymouth residents, not to stir up the Massachusetts Colony. The Governor might burn his copy if he so chose.

Disappointed as he was by failure to prick the conscience of the Colony, the crusader was even more disturbed by an act of the Plymouth Elders just then. After an interview with Governor Bradford, he came raging in to Mary.

"Persecution starts here now! Plymouth is like Boston as one pea is like another. For certain beliefs which were considered mad, they have exiled a citizen of this town. In all this region there is no respect for liberty of conscience!"

Mary watched him wistfully. "What wouldst do, my husband, were the wish of thy heart granted?"

Quick came the answer. "I would join a settlement where each man might think and worship as he chose. Aye, and do as he chose, also, save that he not interfere with others."

After this episode it was a great relief to hear unexpectedly that he was wanted back at the Salem church. The place of Teacher had never been filled and he was glad to go. Mary was even happier about the change. It filled to the brim her new cup of bliss. A small daughter was born just a few weeks before they started north and her parents called her Mary in honor of her mother. The baby shared the warm welcome at Salem and comforted her mother whenever Roger was away on his trading trips.

One afternoon Mr. Skelton's stocky figure hurried down the grassy path to Roger's house. The latter was just back from a long journey into the Narragansett country and was busy cleaning his high leather boots just outside the door. Sitting near him, with the baby in her lap, Mary was making a tiny dress from a piece of woolen cloth just received from the weaver.

After a hasty greeting, the minister burst out, "Word has just come up from Boston of a ship arriving there. Two men of whom you have oft spoken, Mr. Williams, have landed—Mr. John Cotton and Mr. Thomas Hooker."

Joy lighted Roger's face. "Praise God they be come! Men of great learning and godliness are they. This is the best news I have heard since young John Winthrop came to these shores more than a year since."

Mr. Skelton nervously smoothed down his wide-skirted tunic. "Doubtless they are such," he replied in a grudging tone, "but I doubt if they be willing that our church be independent of Boston."

When he finally saw Hooker and John Cotton, Roger was touched at the personal warmth of their greeting. Yet Cotton at once took his young admirer to task. His agitation about paying Indians for land, his Separatist stand, his criticism of the Massachusetts government—well! "It is unquiet and unlamblike of you, Mr. Williams, to question the righteous men of this Colony."

Roger sounded young John Winthrop on the situation. The two were always happy to meet together, always regretful that their meetings had been so infrequent since John joined his father in America. But the Governor's son was full of warnings for his friend. Couldn't he accept things as they were?

Not he. A new tyranny over men's thoughts was now in the making at Boston. There a monthly meeting was attended by every minister in the Colony. What they were doing was to frame a complete doctrine which every church member was to believe.

Roger, who had a great deal of influence in Salem, was ardently opposing this attempt to rule the very soul.

"What I love in thee, friend Williams," Richard Waterman said to him, "is that thou hast no fear. Too many shudder before the power of the Massachusetts Bay Company."

During the next twelve months that power was turned full against the fearless young man.

In December 1633, the year he returned to Salem, he was brought before the General Court and warned to keep his opinions to himself. But to a crusader that was impossible. A fresh cause for battle appeared the very next spring. Officials of the Bay Company demanded an oath of loyalty to the Court which took precedence over the oath to Charles First. Against this illegal oath Roger campaigned so ardently that finally it was dropped.

When a day of penitence was declared in the autumn of 1634, the Salem Teacher preached a startling sermon. In it he discussed at length eight major sins committed by Massachusetts. His friends trembled for his safety. But a summons before the Council resulted only in giving him a year's grace for repentance of his wild notions. John Cotton volunteered to convert this man, again called by Hooker "so divinely mad." He must learn to co-operate with the authorities instead of fighting them.

In spite of fatiguing conflict, Roger prospered in both friendship and trade. He was now employing part of the time a boy brought over as an indentured servant by Richard Waterman. Young Thomas Angell looked after Mary and the children whenever Roger went on a long expedition. By this time the trader had explored most of the territory now included in Massachusetts, Connecticut, and Rhode Island. He was welcomed by all the tribes as a friend. At a special conference with the wise old sachem of the Narragansetts, Canonicus, he made a plan for the future. If he should be exiled by Massachusetts, he wished to buy land near Narragansett Bay. Cordially Canonicus made a verbal treaty with him for such a purchase.

1635 was marked by new tensions. Massachusetts had been under fire in England for some time. Now it was rumored that a royal governor might be sent over to rule the Colony. The Bay Company resolved to resist such a move by force. The fort was manned and on a height overlooking the village of Boston a beacon was placed, to be lighted by watchers whenever a vessel approached. Ever since, the elevation, now in the heart of the city, has been called Beacon Hill.

Salem's loyalty to its unruly Teacher suddenly began to be undermined. For a new issue had come up. The town had petitioned the General Court for use of Marblehead Point as a common pasture land. Promptly the Court replied that consent depended on dismissal of Roger Williams from the church. Time and again he had been summoned to Boston for warnings and reproof. In August of that year he was required to meet his mentor, John Cotton, in a series of public discussions.

These were memorable debates. It was a shock to the university men among the Boston leaders to find their youthful enemy so brilliant and learned. He was deeply read in all the social theories of radical Puritans. John Cotton began this fencing bout with the tolerant superiority of an expert toward a novice. Soon he found himself hard pressed to keep blade in hand.

In his preacher's voice of authority Cotton said, "The civil government is an ordinance of God. Therefore none but members of the church dare be electors."

Like a falcon Roger swooped upon the argument. "Aye, truly some form of civil government accords with God's will toward men. We must learn to live together sociably—else would we prey upon one another like the fish in the sea. But it is the people themselves, Mr. Cotton, not a group of the elect who have all the power to set up what government they wish."

Cotton's lip curled in disdain. "Democracy, I conceive, God never did ordain. His saints must guide the people. Better the commonwealth be fashioned by God's church than to accommodate the church to the civil state."

Roger flung out his hands in passionate protest. "Nay, but the two are separate. Today we do wrong to follow the pattern of ancient Hebrew life. Christ Jesus taught that religion and government must remain apart. What said Christ, Mr. Cotton? 'Render unto Caesar the things which are Caesar's; and unto God the things that are God's.' "

Every time he spoke Roger saw his ideas shape themselves more clearly. He felt himself part of a future in which the common man had rights both as a soul and as a citizen. With all his zeal and skill he tried to pierce the thick armor of the Boston saints to let in a little of the light that blazed in his heart. With Thomas Hooker he could agree on many things. Hooker at least wanted a democratic church controlled by the congregation. But Hooker thought there ought to be just one church to which everyone belonged. When Roger pled for freedom of thought, Hooker shook his head in disapproval. Never, indeed, did the Teacher from Salem meet any but hostile eyes from his audience.

At last the strain told on the young man. The sharp contention, added to hard physical work performed as farmer and trader, wore him out. One evening he collapsed in Mary's arms. Exhaustion was followed by fever and he became seriously ill. Young Angell and Mary were alarmed about him.

His most constant visitor was a liberal-minded Elder named Sharpe. One night the Elder brought bad news. "The officers of the church and even its members are slipping from the rock on which they stood," he said mournfully. "I fear they mean to yield submission to Boston."

Pressure upon the church from citizens and magistrates had proved too great to withstand. Marblehead land was worth a sacrifice. The congregation was not going to ask Roger to resign, but talked of giving up its independence of authority and accepting the control of the Boston church.

Propped up on his pillows, Roger fixed burning eyes on his visitor. The fight was lost then! For the congregation to take this stand at such a moment and for such a reason meant that all hope of disentangling religion from civil matters must be given up. That night the patient's fever rose dangerously. When it subsided a little, he wrote to the Elders that if the church joined itself to the Boston church, he would have to resign his post as Teacher.

Soon afterwards a deputation called to plead with him. He must remain their Teacher. Yet they had to tell him that at a church meeting it was voted to accept the terms required for getting rights to the Marblehead lands. Nor could they deny that the moment Boston took control of the Salem church, the order would come to dismiss the Teacher. On the Sunday following this visitation, Roger sent in a message to the Elders which was more than a mere resignation. He withdrew from the church and from all other churches in America. His career as minister and church member was over.

"My dear one . . ." Mary, kneeling beside the bed after she had read the letter, looked at her husband with tears in her eyes. "I know you feel you must take this step. But I have no will to leave my friends in the Salem church nor give up membership there."

Roger laid his thin hand on her hair. His eyes widened in surprise. Then he closed them and was silent for a long time. When he opened them he was smiling. He had remembered how Sir Edward Coke had received his announcement of entering the ministry. Here now was his own test of how much he believed in freedom for another.

"Thou must not leave the church, Mary," he said softly. "Do as conscience bids thee always."

Now the Bay authorities began a vigorous campaign against their foe. Letters accusing Roger Williams of many wrongs were sent to freemen and church members of Salem. The famous Hugh Peters, just arrived in Boston, was preaching against the rebel with fiery zeal. As he slowly grew better, Roger steeled himself to face what was surely coming.

John Throckmorton came often to discuss the new laws passed by the Massachusetts Assembly. The first one permitted only freemen to vote in any church or town or settlement. The next statute ruled that even a church member who was not a freeman had no franchise within or without the church. The Bay clergy drew up a document called "Model of Church and Civil Power."

Throckmorton went over it with Roger. "Look, Mr. Williams, it says herein that whenever the churches are in doubt about a matter; they should 'consider and consult with the Court.' There you have the two authorities intertwined."

"Aye," Roger burst out with all his old energy, "these men of power would be saints and priests to guide the rest of us, and liberty is dead."

When his friend had gone, Roger climbed down from the loft and went to sit near Mary who was baking bread. "Mary, I have had several letters from Mr. Cotton, Mr. Winthrop, and others, asking that I deny all that I have said against the practices of Boston. Knowing of these recent laws, I have written them that I think more than ever tyranny is come to Massachusetts. Soon they will act against me. Be prepared."

Soon, indeed! On October 8th he was summoned for formal trial before the General Court. It was held at Newtown in Mr. Thomas Hooker's church, a small wooden building with a dirt floor. At one end sat the Governor and his legal adviser. Near him were nine magistrates. Then twenty-five deputies took their seats. Mr. Cotton, Mr. Hooker, Mr. Peters, and several others were there to help question the culprit.

Seated before the rulers of the Holy Commonwealth, Roger wished his friend Sir Edward could see how the English Common Law was being abused. The Governor was both presiding officer and prosecuting attorney. Without specific charge against the accused, his beliefs were held up for examination and attack. One individual after another arose to call them dangerous. Mr. Williams, said they, had won many from allegiance to the Court. He had tried to undermine the Colony's hold on its land by saying the true patent of ownership belonged to the Indians. He defied the magistrates by saying they had power over the outward state of man only, and none in spiritual matters.

At last Roger began his own defense. He had neither counsel nor friend to aid him. There were dark circles under his brilliant eyes. The hands he used so much for dramatic gestures were thin. Sometimes a cough shook his slender frame. Such signs of physical weakness seemed to bring out all the more the magnificent strength of his convictions.

"You in the Bay Colony," he cried passionately, "do use the pattern of Israel for your action. Moses is your leader, not Christ. I do affirm it be against the testimony of Christ Jesus for the civil state to impose upon the soul of the people a religion, a worship, and a ministry. The state should give free and absolute permission of conscience to all men in what is spiritual alone. Ye have lost yourselves! Your breath blows out the candle of liberty in this land."

Until the sun went down the argument continued. When Court adjourned until next day, John Cotton came to stand before the defendant. "Will nothing melt down your rocky strength?" he asked anxiously. "If you yield not in some things, Mr. Williams, nothing can save you from banishment."

John Winthrop, the former Governor, repeated this warning. He walked out of the church with his old friend and Roger felt the man's real, but helpless, concern.

That evening at the house where he was given food and a bed, young John Winthrop came to see him. He had just landed after many months in England and the two friends discussed his experiences as eagerly as though no discord lay between them. Winthrop had come back with a commission to found a new Colony in Connecticut and serve as Governor for a year.

"Many inquired after you," smiled John. "Sir William Masham is your good friend."

Roger's face lit up. "They do not agree with all I think," he remarked, "but I doubt they will be pleased with my banishment from here."

Young Winthrop looked pained. "Perchance tomorrow you will find a means of compromise."

Here was no champion of the difficult cause of liberty! Roger had always known it and realized that now his friend was less than ever likely to speak out for him. While in England, Winthrop had married Hugh Peters' step-daughter. Peters was mentioned as the likely head of the Salem church and wished to make an example of this firebrand.

Next day the argument began again. Roger's rocky strength did not give way. At last, in despair of breaking him down, the Court proclaimed his sentence. He was to be banished from the Colony in six weeks' time. With that news he returned to Mary.

As Roger put it, "Some fifty good men did what they thought was just." But that powerful group did not represent the thousands of families scattered over Massachusetts. Reports of the Court sentence rippled through the Colony leaving shock and indignation behind. From all corners appeals were sent. Officials were told that Mr. Williams had by no means recovered from his illness and that his wife was expecting another child. To send that pair from their home in November with a little girl of two and a newborn infant would be murder. Was this inspired Teacher and good neighbor not worth a little mercy? Both the Winthrops pled against the sentence. And suddenly a strong new voice joined the chorus.

One day a small craft called a pinnace tacked smartly into Salem harbor. From it stepped a young man with an escort of men from Boston. Even as his foot touched shore, excitement and wonder ran before him through the town. Tall, handsomely dressed, with a face of rare beauty framed in golden-brown curls falling from under his wide plumed hat, he stood out among the sober Puritans like a rose in a vase of tansy. The escort said the visitor was to see Mr. Endicott. But the name on the stranger's own lips was Roger Williams. Would someone bring Mr. Williams to Mr. Endicott's house at once?

When Thomas Angell burst in with the message, Roger gasped in astonishment. Instantly he was tossed back to a day in London when he had watched the courtiers supporting the Crown file from the King's council room. Roger remembered clearest of all the Comptroller of the King's Household, Sir Henry Vane. Even then he had learned that the royal official had begot a strange son, a liberal, a Puritan, an opposer of arbitrary power. Roger had heard that this youngster had come to America on the same ship with John Winthrop, Junior, but had been too troubled to give him a moment's thought. Hastening to the Endicott house, Roger grasped the hand of Harry Vane.

"Mr. Williams!" Sympathy warmed the handsome, boyish face. "I land in Boston only to learn of your sentence of banishment. When I did discover the cause, I sorrowed that so ardent an apostle of liberty should be cast out."

Interrupted then by Roger's murmur of thanks, Vane said quickly, "I would learn more of these beliefs which have cost you so dear. What I know of them seems the very truth."

Roger, however, had eager questions of his own—about events

in the homeland and about the friends whom Winthrop had not mentioned.

"Mr. Williams," said the youth, "you speak of my father's opponents. I knew them first as the target of his good round oaths." Harry Vane laughed gaily, showing his fine white teeth. "Lately, however, I have met these persons face to face and hope to call them friends, also."

His first report made Roger's cheek turn pale. Sir Edward Coke had died at Stoke Poges, hard-working to the last. Oliver Cromwell, Mr. Hampden, and John Pym were organizing resistance to the King's demands. Never summoning Parliament, Charles ruled alone. He was trying to build a fleet and his opponents watched his every move. Scotland worked to establish a Presbyterian National Church, a substitute for democracy. Archbishop Laud still made England a place of suffering for Puritans.

Before their talk ended, both Roger and Harry felt a deep mutual sympathy. The latter asked permission to visit Roger's home for more discussion, and Roger went away marveling that a family of worldly aristocrats could have produced this wonderful boy.

Roger always believed that it was Vane's intercession which finally brought reprieve to the Williams family. The Court sent word that not until the next spring was the sentence of banishment to take effect. Mary needed that much ease of mind. For shortly after the letter came she gave birth to another little daughter. The stout-hearted parents named her Freeborne.

Although fever and coughing still kept Roger in bed many hours each day, his house was a center of lively discussion that late autumn. Candles on the stretcher table and light from crackling logs shone on earnest faces. Harry Vane, sprawling on a wooden bench with careless grace, seemed most eager of all.

"Mr. Williams, 'tis plain you mislike the royal rule in England without check of Parliament, and like not much better the priest rule of Massachusetts. What then judge you to be a good state?"

He listened intently as Roger outlined his ideas. In the first place, state and local governments must serve the people—defend them against enemies within and without, protect individual rights, and curb personal liberty only for public good.

"But secondly," said Roger, "neither the form of government nor its laws should ever be too fixed and hard. Men change. Circumstances change. So must the people's government."

One evening with a toss of his curls Vane cried, "Let us talk of the future." He had been excited to learn that his new friend was planning to buy land in the Narragansett country. "Since you have made treaties with the Indians, Mr. Williams, why could you not start a settlement of your own? There you could set up a government where liberty might live."

Roger gave him a startled look. "I had dreamed only of a home, unfettered by priestly rules, where I might work with the Indians."

With one voice John Throckmorton and Richard Waterman declared, "If you start a home, others will follow you."

Somehow Boston authorities learned of the meetings at Roger's house. It was reported to them that at least twenty people were ready to go with the banished man to found a new state. In a fury of indignation, the Governor and his Assistants decided that so dangerous a person must be deported to England. They swore out a warrant for his arrest and sent the summons up to Salem.

To Mary Williams the arrival of this message was the crack of doom. "Oh, my husband," she cried in an anguished voice, "is this the end of our efforts and struggles?"

"I shall refuse to go on the grounds of health," he answered quickly. But his brow was furrowed with anxiety.

A doctor's certificate declaring Mr. Williams unable to travel was returned to the Governor, together with a packet of protesting letters. Over the little house in Salem, December clouds hung not so thick as the shadow of this new threat. One day a messenger arrived with a letter. After he had had a cup of tea and departed, Roger broke the seal.

"Quick, my husband, what is it?" Mary kneeled beside him in terror.

"Good John Winthrop, my friend, warns me of peril," he said. "The present Governor is sending up a pinnace with fourteen armed men under a captain to fetch me down to the ship for England."

Mary gave a little shriek. "Then all is lost!"

Roger's body was tense as a spring. He pressed his wife close and in grim silence stared at the fire. Then he held her away from him to look into her true eyes. "Mary, a plan of escape has come to me."

When she heard what it was, she clung to him, sobbing that he was too ill to try it. But with a hand stroking her hair, he said, "Let us remember the Psalmist's words, 'Thou shalt not be afraid for the terror by night, nor for the arrow that flieth by day.'"

Suddenly he sprang to his feet. "I must see several men who will help me set my affairs in order." Flinging his woolen cloak about him, he turned at the door and looked back. His face held a light Mary was long to remember.

"All is not lost, dear wife. Should I outwit these servants of Jehovah and preserve my liberty, I may undertake a great adventure for the Lord."

8

A SHIVERING fox stopped dead to watch him. Three weary eagles, flapping sleet-covered wings, looked down upon him—a strange, two-legged creature moving laboriously through trackless snow. Bent almost double to cleave the roaring wind, he staggered across the rocky plateau to the edge of the forest.

Clinging to the lee side of a mammoth pine tree, he stood coughing and panting with fatigue. After a moment he peered into the woods. Amid tumbled boulders, they dropped downward sharply into a deep ravine.

"Thomas!" he called. "Thomas Angell!"

"Aye, Mr. Williams!" A reassuring shout came up. "I've found the ledge and water below."

Cautiously Roger moved down the slope. At his third step the snow surface, which looked so firm, gave way and he plunged waist deep into a hole. His knee struck a huge buried stone. Stunned by the severe jar, he had to wait some moments before he could shift his pack and continue the descent.

Like a steadying hand, the boy's cheerful voice reached up. "Bear to the right a bit, sir! You're almost there."

Now the man could see the level shelf half way down the deep gully. On it a heap of mighty rocks leaned upon one another in such a way as to form a tent-like structure, roofed above and carpeted with dry leaves. Just outside Thomas was kneeling before a well-heaped pile of wood. With steel and flint he was trying to get a spark to light a dry leaf.

"Hah, she's starting!" Thomas flicked a glance at the snow-covered figure edging between the rocks. By the time Roger had dropped his pack in the cave and opened it, a fire was roaring on the flat surface outside.

Swiftly the man drew from his pack an iron pot, emptied into it the gourd Angell had filled at the creek below, and set it carefully on the coals.

"Well done, lad!" he said, smiling. "We shall sup on Indian mush."

With a look of grave anxiety at his companion, the boy said, "You are limping, sir, and tremble with the cold. Watch here by the fire and I shall cut some pine branches for our beds."

It was now dusk. The man could barely follow the departing figure blending with the forest shadows. Yet Thomas remained so near that the sawing of his knife along the branches seemed loud. Warming his back at the fire, Roger shaded his eyes to see better.

With the shift of a burning log, a sudden flame shot up to fling brilliant light over the tree which Thomas had climbed. Roger's pulse gave a leap. Wasn't there a strange, dark shape crouched in the branches above the boy? The firelight caught in two round spots of gleaming green. It was a mountain cat ready to spring!

Roger swooped upon the musket propped against the cave. With practiced movements he primed the pan with powder from the powder horn, checked lead and flint, and, stepping forward, took aim. A warning scream from the animal, the gun's roar, and the crash of a falling weight snapping off tree limbs seemed parts of one multiple sound.

"Thomas!"

Roger's cry was topped by another animal scream. At him out of the dark came a leaping horror with eyes and teeth agleam. There was no time to prime and fire. Only a second to swing the gun like a club and bring it down with an impact that made him stagger. Almost in the coals the cat fell sprawling. One glance at the crushed skull and the gaping chest wound told Roger he was dead.

Dragging the beast to one side, he hurried to the tree. "Thomas!" he called again.

There was no answer. A huddled figure lay prone in the snow. At the touch of his trembling fingers, however, the boy sat up and his hands flew to his head. In answer to Roger's anxious question, he mumbled that he must have been stunned in falling. With a sheepish laugh he struggled to his feet. Then memory came back and he clutched the arm supporting him.

" 'Ods Wounds, sir, the cat!"

"Aye. 'Twas a narrow moment. He lies there!"

Roger watched his companion closely to be certain he had received no injury. But the boy's swift actions were reassuring. He stooped over the carcass with astonished and admiring cries, then whirled upon Roger with choked words of gratitude. Warned by a hissing from the fire, he rescued the boiling pot, piled on more logs, and then went to gather up the pine branches he had cut. Hardly had he heaped them in the cave and spread the blankets down, when Roger collapsed upon the bed. His strength was gone.

At dawn next morning the two sat talking of the route they

were to follow. They had covered half the distance from Salem to Sowams on the northeast shore of Narragansett Bay. By night they would reach an Indian village well known to Roger and, the next night, Sowams.

"If the sachem, Massasoit, will shelter me—and I count upon his kindness—you must return at once to Salem, Thomas. Mr. Waterman said you were to look after Mrs. Williams and the children."

The boy nodded. "Ye be a wonder for knowing the way in this wild land, Mr. Williams. Another would be lost. And a prize hunter, too. Unless that first shot went true, the beast would have clawed me well."

Often during those two days of crossing icy creeks, climbing cliffs, and threading snowy forest trails, the sick man felt that only prayer kept him on his feet. Fever burned in his veins. Muscles ached and the injured knee pained at every step. Striding ahead, young Angell cheered him on. At sunset on the last day the trail widened and grew smoother. Landmarks Roger had noted on many other trips to see Massasoit began to appear and hope spurred him on.

Suddenly Thomas stopped and stiffened. Over his head Roger saw outlined against the lemon patch of sky at the forest edge a brave wrapped in beaver skins. The bow in his hand was taut and the arrow aimed and ready. From befogged depths of memory Roger brought up three Indian words and hurled them at the threatening figure.

"*Nummauchem, Nétop. Neàthop.*"

As he heard the hoarse voice crying, "I am sick, friend. I am hungry," the Indian dropped his bow and came forward. A close look at the speaker ended in a smile of recognition.

"Welcome, friend," he said. "I lead you to the sachem's tepee!"

What happened after that remained forever blank to the exhausted traveler. When he opened his eyes again it was in blissful relaxation. He was lying on something soft. Dim daylight, filtered through smoky air, showed him clay-filled logs overhead. His ears caught the sound of voices and clatter. Presently a dark face bent over him and a powerful hand shifted his head, while something hot in an earthen bowl was pressed against his lips. He drank and sank immediately into sleep. But with him he took a comforting certainty. He was in the house of Massasoit. At last he had warmth, care, rest, and food.

Weeks passed before Roger could sit up. When at last he staggered out of doors, the cold damp air brought him the smell of spring. One of the children ran into the woods and brought back for him a handful of arbutus. As he sniffed the exquisite fragrance, strength seemed to seep back into his veins.

Next day a runner brought a letter from Mary. She reported that all was well. Thomas Angell had returned and was doing his part, and no vengeance had been wreaked on the wife of Boston's escaped culprit. As he finished reading, Roger became aware that he was ringed around by squaws, children, and youths, all gazing at him curiously.

Smiling at their eagerness for news, he said, "Wife well. Children well. They come when I build house."

That was what he wished to do immediately. Before he was really fit to travel he had himself paddled over to the western mainland where the Narragansett country began. On the trip he noted every detail of the landscape—the rocky or marshy shore line, the forest-covered hills. The great bay, gored out of the land by the ocean's might, was dotted with islands large and small. Up several rivers rushed the tide to gnaw coves out of the inland shores.

As the Indians helped him over the icy trail leading to the winter quarters of Canonicus, Roger felt his fever coming up again. Dishes of boiled acorns and mush had not built up his strength. It was all he could do, after arriving at the dark, smoky hovel which served for royal residence, to stand through the sachem's ceremony of welcome. For many days, wrapped in wolf skins, he lay near the fire, longing for medicine and care. But the moment he was walking about again, Canonicus asked him to attend a formal council. He had expected the summons. For Massasoit had told him a dispute had arisen between himself and the Narragansetts.

Now he heard the Narragansett version of the argument. At one end of the tepee on an enormous bear rug the chief sat cross-legged. Beside him with a fox skin flung over his bare shoulders sat the magnificent young prince, Miantonomo, the sachem's nephew. As the talk began, the Englishman realized the curtain was rising on a typical Indian intrigue.

Massasoit had recently put himself under the protection of Plymouth. It was a first step toward making himself independent of the Narragansetts. But he could not get free from Narragansett authority without breaking established treaties. This Canonicus would not tolerate. He said Massasoit was heading straight for war. But since Roger Williams was friendly to both parties, perhaps he would undertake to arbitrate the difficulty.

Roger thanked the sachem for the honor. Intuition told him

that the mission would open up a new career of service. For the next fortnight he went back and forth along the trails, sat at council meetings, smoked the pipe of peace, and neither heard nor spoke a word of English. He was treated with all the ceremony due a sachem, and filled the role by giving each discussion his loving thought. Never by look or gesture did he betray any sense of strangeness or discomfort.

His reward was complete success in the mission. Massasoit was mollified and won over to compromise. In the end he was so pleased by the outcome that he gave Roger a tract of land on the east bank of the Seekonk River, and set his mark on the deed drawn up by the recipient. Furthermore, he joined with the Narragansett sachems in appointing Roger official agent and interpreter between all the New England tribes and the English governments.

"Our hearts see your goodness," said Canonicus at the end of the conference. "Your tongue is not cleft and truth is on your lips. Never do you set up white men as gods."

At the Indian camp in the Plymouth territory Roger received many letters and several visitors. Both the Winthrops wrote of their relief that he had survived the terrible winter. They reported many upheavals in Massachusetts. Harry Vane had been elected Governor. A strange woman named Anne Hutchinson, who had recently reached Boston with her husband and children, was worrying the Elders. Although Vane and even Cotton were sympathetic with her, the meetings she had begun to hold at her own house and her strange doctrines offended the authorities.

John Cotton and Thomas Hooker had split. What was the soul's state before being filled with faith? That question wrecked their friendship. Hooker was going down into the Connecticut Valley to start a settlement and church. Most of the members of his own church, with others from Dorchester and Watertown, were moving with him. They wanted a free church controlled by its own congregation.

Mary wrote that Roger's mother had died and left him a legacy. When he got it and also money from the man who had bought his Indian trade at Salem, he would have ample funds to start the new home. As soon as it was ready, she would come with the children.

With strength returned and fresh hope in his heart, Roger set about planning with Massasoit the building of his house. Hardly had these conversations begun when a man came into camp asking to see him. He proved to be one John Smith, a miller from Dorchester, who had also been banished.

"Mr. Williams," said he anxiously, "when I had word from friends in Salem that you were starting a home outside Massachusetts, I set out at once to join you. Could we not help one another? And I brought with me a poor young fellow named Francis Wickes, who would help us and settle close by."

Smith also said that a penniless wanderer named William Harris was on his way to discuss the same possibility of a refuge. Roger gave his visitor refreshment and went off by himself to reflect about this unexpected turn of events. Since he always had meant to bring Thomas Angell along, there would be five men ready to settle a new place together. Fate was taking a hand. Not just a home for his family, but a settlement, as Harry Vane had suggested—that was what loomed ahead of him. Excitement stole through his veins. Now perhaps he could build a place where men could be free in their thoughts and yet learn to live together in mutual peace.

One look at his face and Smith, the miller, knew their fates were joined. William Harris proved to be a sullen fellow, but one quite ready to work. When Thomas Angell came from Salem, bringing spades and axes, the party set off.

In late April the birds, beavers, fish, and otters found their domain along the Seekonk River rudely invaded. Blows of the ax, the rhythmic thud of spade and hoe split the forest silence. One afternoon another man walked up and asked to join the group. He was Joshua Verin, a roper. When they rested around the open fire at twilight, Roger talked to them about the thoughts which filled his mind day and night. His heart was high with the hope of this new free society.

But just when most of the crops were sown, that hope was felled at a blow. Into camp an Indian brought a letter to Roger from the new Governor of Plymouth, Edward Winslow. Regretfully the Governor said that the grant from Massasoit on the Seekonk River was within Plymouth territory. Plymouth was not willing to accept within its borders exiles from Massachusetts. Therefore Mr. Williams would have to move farther west.

A second banishment! Crops planted for nothing! Roger spent hours in bitter reflection. When at last he was calm, however, he decided to be grateful to Plymouth's Governor. A new colony founded in freedom must, indeed, take root in virgin soil.

Next morning he broke the news to his companions in a tone of cheerful resolution. He declared protest was a waste of time. Within a few hours they had packed up all their belongings and were off in their canoes to find a new site. Down the Seekonk

River they sped with the turning tide.

Near its mouth they swept close to shore. Suddenly a call came over the water. Roger saw an Indian poised, tall and lithe, on the top of a rock near the beach. "What cheer, friend?" he called.

"We seek a home," Roger shouted back, smiling.

A little below that rock another stream joined the Seekonk to form the Great Salt River which was really an arm of the Bay. They decided to push up the river. When on the western bank they saw a wide clearing left by the Indians, they landed to explore.

"Here be a kind of peninsula between rivers," said William Harris.

In a meadow crossed by clear fresh streams was a fine spring. Behind the level strip to the east and also to the north rose forest-covered hills. Water and woods and fields already cleared! It looked promising.

"Let us camp here," said Roger. "Tomorrow I shall visit Canonicus of the Narragansetts, who own this land. Doubtless he will let us stay."

In three days he was back. Canonicus, delighted to have his friend for neighbor, had granted him by verbal treaty the entire peninsula between the Moshassuck and Woonsquatucket Rivers, and also a tract running south on the western shore of the Bay. The chief insisted that Roger had already paid for the land in services. Cheers greeted the news. In turn the pioneers reported wild game and strawberries in the woods, and clam beds in the salty shallows along the shore.

The four men and two boys climbed the hill back of the spring. From the crest between the trees they could see salt marshes to the west and out toward the bay, and many islands covered with coarse grass. "Pasture for our cattle!" they cried with one voice.

In silence Roger gave a prayer of thanksgiving. Then he said, "Let us call this place New Providence. For surely we have been led here by divine guidance."

Work started at once. First the fields were spaded and sown. Next lumber was cut for building. As they gathered around a community fire for the evening meal, everybody discussed the village to be. The street would follow along the east bank of the Moshassuck River and ten-acre lots would run straight back from street to hilltop, with houses standing snugly close together in a row. Each resident would also have six acres of woodland lying east of the town. As for pastures, these might be held in common at first.

There was a glow in Roger's heart as he made these assignments to the sturdy but penniless refugees about him. Yet, as he discussed terms, he felt the shrewd black eyes of William Harris fixed upon him in sly calculation.

"This tract was given me by that great sachem, Canonicus, and his nephew, Miantonomo, for many services and gifts from me. I gladly share it with each of you without payment. Yet for justice I ask only that in time thirty shillings be paid into a central fund by each comer and that from such sums thirty pounds to reimburse me for divers outlay be paid to me."

Without dissenting voice, all agreed that the proprietor's terms were generous in the extreme.

Also by common consent it was decided that Roger's house was to be on the lot nearest the spring. Before the rough foundations were laid several other men arrived to share the bounty of this new settlement.

As the corn shoots pushed up green above the earth, Roger set out to weave a web of peace with neighboring Indians—all small tribes subordinate to the Narragansetts. From each he won a pledge of friendship. Meanwhile he was slowly and carefully starting the wheels of government.

"It would seem a good thing," he told his companions, "that each and all meet together every fortnight to settle our problems by common consent. There must be a watch to guard the crops against wild animals and to keep roving heathen from tools and provisions. That must be divided amongst us. And other things must be settled."

At first the meetings were mere general discussions. Simple rules were verbally agreed to and no one kept minutes. Presently, as the group grew larger, the meetings took on a little more formality. With some ceremony the pioneers incorporated themselves into a town fellowship and set a fine upon anyone who was late to the conference. As the weeks drew on, the leader thought it was time to make clear the basis of the government he hoped to establish.

"Here in New Providence," he said one day to the assembled settlers, "we are making a refuge for men of tender conscience. There must be full liberty for each to walk his own path to God."

"Aye," approved John Smith in a deep voice, "many of us have suffered for lack of such liberty in the Massachusetts Bay Colony and in Plymouth also. Let us have a way of freedom here."

With everyone agreed on that great principle, with everyone hard at work to build homes and cultivate crops, with several cows, driven down from Massachusetts, grazing on the pasture, and Indian visitors arriving to bring gifts and cast curious eyes at the settlers, New Providence was humming with activity. Suddenly, sharp as a rifle's crack, came a warning from the savage world surrounding the little camp at the forest's edge.

Early one morning, as Roger was hoeing in his cornfield, an Indian raced up the hill from the river bank where he had left his canoe. Breathlessly he panted out an alarming tale. A trader living on Block Island, some distance out to sea, had been murdered by a band of Pequot Indians. His two boys and all his goods were carried off. Another trader had brought the corpse to the Narragansett camp and threatened revenge. Canonicus was greatly agitated. The Pequots, ancient enemies, had been subdued by the more powerful tribe. They could not be allowed to break the peace between their superiors and the English. Should war be declared against them by the Narragansetts? The sachem wished to see Roger Williams at once.

"I come," said Roger.

In half an hour he had told the others, given directions, and set off. Tirelessly two Indians paddled the long miles across the bay. When at last he had reached the house of Canonicus and heard the details of the crime, he asked for a messenger to take word of it to Governor Harry Vane.

When he had finished the letter and returned to the council, he found Miantonomo dressed in full war regalia. "I go to avenge wrong," stated the young prince. "Pequots pay in blood for evil deeds."

In horror Roger foresaw that battle in the forest. It was sure to threaten the safety of white men in the neighborhood. Moreover, violence and treachery went hand in hand among the savages. It was conceivable that the Pequots might try to persuade the Narragansetts that they had been wronged by the trader and that all English were enemies. Earnestly he urged Miantonomo to delay action. But the haughty scorn of the brave's refusal warned him that protest was useless.

Next morning the expedition set off. Two hundred fighters, hideous in war paint, armed with spears, bows, and arrows, assembled on the shore. Thirty at a time, they took their places in long canoes and with blood-curdling yells swept off toward the south.

Once more Roger sent a message to Governor Vane. Reporting Miantonomo's invasion of the Pequot country, he begged the magistrates to keep calm and work for peace. In a letter to young John Winthrop, which a passing trader offered to deliver, he repeated the plea. All the peacemaker could do then was to pray with Canonicus and assure him of his wish to help. Oppressed with anxiety, he returned to New Providence.

As the Indian paddlers landed him on the river beach, Roger looked about with an upsurge of joy. The mysterious horrors of the savage realm dropped away. Here before him a stretch of meadow was changing into the semblance of a village. Half-finished houses were actually standing side by side along the river path. Each had a frame of solid oak set on a low foundation. Some already had chimneys standing tall and firm. Behind the houses stood fields of corn glistening in the sun.

When the villagers dropped their tools and rushed at him for news, he had to say soberly, "No man may tell the outcome of this sorrowful affair."

But for the moment dread was swept away by interest in the scene before him. The others had been working on his house and he surveyed it with proud eyes. It was the largest of all. Yet it boasted only two rooms—the "fire room" on the ground floor and the "chamber" or sleeping apartment above. As soon as chimney and roof were finished, Roger wrote his wife to come as quickly as she could. Already Joshua Verin's wife had joined him and the Smith family was on its way.

Those days of preparation were filled to the brim. At dawn Roger was at work in the fields. Later, with the help of Thomas Angell, he turned cabinetmaker to fashion cradles, a huge oaken chest for clothes, a long stretcher table, and a few chairs and benches.

To John Smith who dropped in to admire his handiwork he said impatiently, "These are bare necessities. Better things I cannot buy until my trade is good again. The business I sold in Salem has not yet been paid for and I cannot make a pittance until this threat of war has disappeared, nor till I find some means of export."

Smith groaned sympathetically. "Aye, those noble saints of Boston do well to refuse you use of their good harbor. But one day ships will anchor here to take your furs and bring us goods."

Looking up from his work of fitting a peg into the table, Roger said soberly, "Meanwhile I must depend on corn and cabbages and pease from my fields to feed us through the winter."

But with Mary he could manage somehow! When she first stepped across the threshold of the big, solid house, Roger watched her face in a passion of eagerness. Did she like it? Would she be happy here?

After a breathless glance around, she turned an exultant face to Roger. "Our home!" she cried. All the long months of loneliness gave eloquence to those two words. "Oh, husband, now we shall really *live!*"

It was rich reward for all his labor. With baby Freeborne in his arms and little Mary clinging to his tunic, he gazed at her with speechless love. Yet her word *live* struck chill to his bones. Death stalked close. In the Pequot country storms of hate were blowing up. Whatever happened, he, the interpreter and chosen agent of the Narragansetts, would be in the center of the whirlwind.

Before a month was up the first rumble of thunder was in their ears.

9

AFTER supper one evening when the children were in bed, Roger and Mary were comparing notes on the long period of their separation. Seated on a bench outside the house, they spoke in low tones to accord with the twilight hush. Down by the river a frog orchestra was just tuning up. Behind them a little sea breeze rustled the starched banners of the corn. From Joshua Verin's hut next door came a boy's treble voice protesting against going to bed.

Mary looked about as if wishing she could trust the peaceful scene. "Roger, amongst all the savage chieftains in whom dost thou place most faith?"

"In Canonicus and Miantonomo," was the prompt reply. "They are noble chieftains and their people are peaceable by nature."

"And yet thou art anxious!"

"Aye. The Pequots may persuade them to false thoughts. Besides, who trusts the Massachusetts Bay officers? Not I! Mr. Harry Vane is ringed about with men who care nothing for these heathen. They might—"

He broke off with a low cry. Springing up, the two saw a man hurrying toward them along the road. He was John Smith who had gone to Plymouth for supplies. He must have news.

"Mr. Williams," panted the miller, "something has happened on Block Island where the trader was murdered. From my boat I saw a cloud of smoke over the place as if fields and huts were burning. It is the work of men sent by the magistrates of Boston. I heard of their expedition when I was in Plymouth."

It was several days before more details could be had. Then it was learned that John Endicott of Salem had landed a force of eighty men on Block Island. After killing all the Indians who had not fled, after burning their huts and crops, the troops sailed into Pequot Harbor on the coast southwest of Providence. In that section Endicott was burning everything he could find. Yet he had met no Pequot forces to fight.

At the fortnightly meeting of Providence men, a hot discussion of these events took place. William Harris shouted, " 'Tis well done! The murdering heathen must be destroyed before they kill us all!"

Roger declared Christians should act otherwise. All the sachems should have been gathered in formal council. Then the English, supported by the Narragansetts and all their tributaries who wanted peace, could have forced the Pequots to yield up the actual murderers for punishment.

"Burning the heathen families' supply of corn for winter doth only stir up feelings of revenge!" he cried.

Not long after that discussion he went again to see Canonicus. A new and frightening situation was laid bare. The Pequots were forming a league to wipe out the English in a terrible massacre. Already the cruel Mohawks living near the Hudson River had agreed to become members. Some smaller tribes had joined. Canonicus admitted that he was sorely tempted himself to link the fate of his people with his race. For one thing, he, as chief of the most important New England tribe, had to be on the winning side. Endicott's expedition had meant no defeat for the Pequots. Burning cornfields was child's play. Lately many settlers in Connecticut had been slain by Pequots and the murders had gone unavenged in blood. Perhaps the English were weak in war.

"Never would we harm you, our friend," said Canonicus in conclusion. "But other English not friends."

Roger had listened in mounting terror. With a mighty effort at composure, he said firmly, "Set your face against this evil, great chief. No gain comes from wrongdoing. I shall pray to our Lord who brought love into the world that you remain friends with my brothers."

Well he knew that if the Narragansetts joined the league, every Indian in New England would rise against the colonists. His soul cried out to all forces for good to hold back such a doom.

On returning to New Providence he sped an account of the

situation to Governor Vane. Reports had come back that disgust was general over the Endicott expedition. The troops had returned to Massachusetts without the murderers, without hostages or even wampum to repay the great cost of the undertaking. Endicott had succeeded only in arousing among all the tribes a hatred which terrified the colonists.

Every man in Providence carried his musket to the fields those days. It was harvest time. Women and even children helped to bring in pumpkins to the root cellars and to shuck the corn.

Roger was piling corn into an Indian basket one morning when he heard his name shouted. A man he had never seen before was being directed toward him by William Harris. In another moment Roger was tearing open a sealed paper brought him by the stranger from Governor Vane.

The amazing document was a commission from the very government which had banished Roger Williams. He was appointed ambassador to prevent the formation of the Indian league. Neither protection nor reward was offered. Yet he was asked to drop everything and go at once to demand a conference in the name of Massachusetts. There was not a moment to be lost.

In half an hour the diplomat was on his way. Mary had packed a change of stockings and a bit of food. She had listened carefully to his directions about the harvest. But as she watched him hurrying down to the river, she stood frozen with anxiety.

Would she ever see him again? First, the dangerous crossing of the bay, whipped to fury by a rising wind. Then the peril of going alone into a camp of savages grown hostile and suspicious. And this at the request of a government which had exiled him as a dangerous enemy! Clutching the baby convulsively, she tried to pray.

Down the river Roger's boat was scudding before its little sail. He sat at the home-made tiller, gathering himself for the mighty physical effort ahead where the white caps were tossing. To tack across the bay would be the trickiest sailing he had ever tried.

For years the memory of that trip stood out clear. As he reached open water, the force of the wind tossed the little craft about like a chip. Roger let the sail drop and picked up his oars. For some time all he could do was to head the prow into the huge waves to prevent its being swamped. Every foot he gained on the oblique course to the far shore cost enormous effort and quick calculation. When at last he moored his boat in a quiet inlet he was too exhausted to move. Limp and soaked with spray, he sat marveling that he had not been drowned. It was some time before he mustered strength to take the trail to the sachem's house.

From the first moment he found an air of tenseness pervading the camp. The youths who escorted him to the tepee told him a conference was going on. He was, therefore, a little prepared for the shock awaiting him. On either side of the sachem were ranged the Pequot ambassadors.

Brief were the mutual salutations. Canonicus in a challenging manner summed up the situation he had been weighing.

"Pequots say all Indians are brothers. They say all white men are enemies to our tribes. Pequots wish all brothers join against enemies."

Roger's voice was low and gentle. "Great sachem knows words spoken in anger are poisoned arrows. Pequot men began this evil. English took wrong way to heal it. Now we must try again. Let all here work for peace."

A cry of derision answered him. One of the Pequot chiefs asked scornfully if burning and killing by the English could be forgiven more easily than the murder of one trader. Why should Indians yield up land to white men who had no love in their hearts? Now let truth be spoken. Hate and war—war to the death—that was what lay between the sons of Manit and the white men from across the sea.

So went the talk. Gravely Roger reminded the warriors that if evil advice prevailed, if war against the English were started, the Indians would lose their lives and their lands. Even were the tribes to win at first, the great King of the English would send men and ships and guns to punish the wicked warriors.

"I speak as friend and my words are not empty," said he in a tone of grave melancholy. "Let us all give up hate and wrongdoing. Let us see how we may make peace."

Canonicus listened as if he had no doubt about his friend. He kept the Pequots from angry interruptions. Yet Roger saw that the Narragansett leaders still believed self-interest lay in joining the league. The conference was full of discord. Roger was not asked to pray with his red-skinned brothers as he so often was.

After the evening meal, topped off by delicious melons, the English agent was assigned to a certain large tent for the night. For a few moments he stayed to sing little songs with the children of Miantonomo. Then, weary to the marrow of his bones, he took a pine torch and stumbled along the rough forest path. Pushing aside the blanket before the opening of the shelter, he stooped to enter. As he lifted the flickering torch to light up the interior, his heart leaped in horror. Only a swift effort of will kept him from turning to flee. For stretched on blankets and squatting against the wall were all the Pequot ambassadors. Their glittering eyes fixed him in wordless threat.

Must he spend the night with these avowed enemies of white men? Surely a knife would be plunged into his breast! Yet in spite of the wild whirl of his thoughts, instinct warned Roger to show no fear. A single sign would be fatal. Either the Pequots would be tempted to dispatch him at once or they would decry him to the Narragansetts as a coward.

With every air of calm he took off hat, boots, and tunic, wrapped himself in his cloak and rolled in a blanket near the door. He was thankful for the draft of fresh air cutting the evil odor of the place. Wasn't it mixed with the smell of blood? Pequot hands were stained with it. They had murdered many settlers and justified their crimes.

Committing himself to God, Roger beat out the torch. In the darkness he tried to remember that real life was eternal and death of no importance. Yet a soft movement near him stopped his breath. Tense and rigid, he listened, listened, listened. Not for an hour did fatigue overpower him with sleep. When he woke at dawn the tent was empty.

For three days the conference continued. Roger went on pleading for peace. He met each argument with quiet common sense. Slowly it became plain that Miantonomo was on his side against the Pequots. Disappointment and fury blazed in the black eyes of the ambassadors. With violent tones and gestures they sprayed hatred over the man whose soft words were undoing their fierce eloquence. For two nights Roger lay in the wigwam by the door waiting for swift death at their hands.

What held them back? Was it fear of the Narragansetts? Roger wondered and thanked God. Then came the last morning of his stay in camp. Silent Hosannahs sang in his heart. For the Narragansett sachems had made their decision. They would not join the league. They would hold to their promise of friendship with the English. Roger laid his hand on the shoulder of Miantonomo and looked with affection into his impenetrable eyes. Canonicus, however, bade his visitor farewell with aloof reserve.

This time the sea was calm, with a little off-shore breeze to fill the sail of the pinnace. Long before night Roger was walking with swift light steps along the crooked path called the Towne Street of New Providence. The sight of his erect, slender figure brought to the settlers a vast relief and to Mary the feeling of being born again.

Work for peace did not stop there. Roger had to take a long trip into Connecticut to confer with Uncas, wily chief of the Mohegan tribe. Uncas was jealous enough of the prosperous Narragansetts to be tempted to join the Pequot league against the combination of Narragansetts and English. It took all Roger's skill to persuade him of the dangerous folly of such a course. But at last he agreed to stay out of the league and even to help the English.

October was more than half over when there took place the formalities of agreement between the Massachusetts Government and the Narragansett sachems. Miantonomo was persuaded to go to Boston with twenty braves to sign the treaty. He himself brought word of the invitation to New Providence.

Roger met his friend like a royal personage. All the officers of the town were presented to him and then Mary welcomed him to the house. She brought him wild grape juice and a honey-sweetened cake for refreshment. As she set plates and cups on the pine table across which her husband and the young prince faced each other, she listened curiously to the strange sound of their talk.

Miantonomo took it for granted that Roger would go with his party to Boston. But Roger shook his head with a little ironic smile. No, he was not going at all.

A quick look of hurt in the black eyes vanished in a haughty stare. "You not wish go with Narragansett warriors?"

"Yes, yes, friend." Roger looked lovingly at the handsome bronzed face. "I would pay much wampum to go. White chiefs in Boston not let me go."

The Indian looked disappointed and troubled. After a long silence he declared that a copy of the treaty would be sent to Roger for translation. Only if he approved would the sachems set their mark upon it. It was Roger they trusted and no other.

After the visitor had gone, Mary asked what they had said. When she learned of the attitude of Boston, her face flamed. "How can savages understand white men? You, the appointed agent of Massachusetts, the one who broke the evil league, are not invited to the peace table! Shame on those men of narrow mind! They are not worthy of your generosity!"

All winter dark shadows hung over New England. It was very cold. Every night wolf traps had to be set at the outskirts of the villages. In the Connecticut Valley the Pequots, aided by the violent Mohawks and by the Niantics, made life a nightmare to isolated farmers. Helpless white families in that district were tortured and murdered without mercy. As these crimes increased with no move on the part of the English to punish them, Canonicus wavered in loyalty. Roger wrote John Winthrop after one of his frequent visits to the Narragansett camp that gifts must be sent to prove the active good will of the treaty signers. Sugar, tools, and clothing were taken to the sachems in Roger's canoe, and he added his own gifts of prayer and preaching and loving counsel.

Before the end of that winter of 1637 everyone knew that New England had to fight the Pequots. If the challenge of their continued murders was not taken up, no tribe would respect the colonists. To help in the preparations for battle, Roger Williams invited Miantonomo to confer with him about the campaign.

With a considerable escort the young sachem arrived in New Providence. In the big house by the spring the braves sat on their fur cloaks in a circle. Miantonomo helped Roger draw up a rough map of the district which is now southern Connecticut. The great Pequot stronghold was Fort Mystic, a short distance north of the coast. With no idea of tactics, the Narragansetts could not suggest how the fort might be taken. But they could mark all the trails, describe every hazard, and insert on the map each creek and river, each hill and valley.

Between sessions Roger was highly amused to observe the astonishment of his guests at the ways of the white family. When he helped Mary at the fireplace to serve the food which she and the maid had prepared, the Narragansetts exchanged glances and grunts. That any man, especially an important leader, would share his wife's menial task was unbelievable. Mary choked down a different kind of question. She wondered whether she could ever again get the room sufficiently aired and cleaned.

"Roger," she said in low-voiced anxiety, "how may I still their appetites? Already they have emptied the pot of hominy and eaten all the clams and three great loaves of bread."

"Be not concerned," he replied, laughing. "Mistress Greene hath kindly sent a pile of oaten cakes and cracked hickory nuts to fill spaces in these brown bellies. Let little Mary pass the dish about the circle."

When the war council was over, Roger fell to work on the notes he had taken. From them he was able to plan a detailed military campaign. This he sent by trusted messenger to John Winthrop, Senior.

The very next day William Harris rushed in with news. "Indians have stormed Saybrook Fort, Mr. Williams!" he cried. "Some English are dead there. 'Tis the boldest vileness yet."

That attack on the outpost founded by young Winthrop was the signal for war. The Massachusetts militia was ready. Boats had been fitted out. Captain Mason, in charge of the expedition, had received Roger's plan of action and off he sailed with his well-armed men.

During those dreadful spring days of 1637, Roger's house was a center of information. Scouts and officers came and went. At last one evening an Indian runner from Miantonomo's camp dashed into the settlement. Behind him rushed the entire population to learn the news at Roger's house. Standing in the doorway, with Mary peering around his shoulder, he listened to the broken words panted out by the young Narragansett. Then he lifted head and hand to fling joy to the crowd.

"Victory!" he shouted. "Fort Mystic has fallen! The first great battle is ours."

Amid cheers and shouts, amid women's grateful sobs and the

shrill whistling of boys, Roger drew the messenger indoors to give him refreshment and learn more of the battle. Outside, the citizens shouted for a meeting of thanksgiving. But when their leader came out again with the runner his face was pale and sad. Gravely he told the people that too many horrors had happened for him to rejoice.

"God hath let the English win," said Roger, "but yet we are guilty. Five hundred human beings slain within the fort—women, children, youths. No mercy was shown by our soldiers. God forgive us all!"

Few there were who shared this sorrow. English successes were cheered to the echo. The militia followed the Pequot forces into a dangerous swamp and there finished the fearful task. That Indian captives were sold into slavery, that hands and scalps were cut from corpses and sent to Boston as mementoes of victory, did not trouble many souls. In vain Roger sent protests to the Massachusetts officials. New England delighted in bloody revenge on the heathen.

It was such unnecessary excesses which Roger attacked. For the essential defeat of the Pequots both he and Mary had worked hard. Once when rumors of Narragansett defeat frightened Canonicus, Roger stayed with him three days to strengthen his loyalty. Meanwhile Mrs. Williams was nursing a wounded soldier whom she kept at the house for weeks. In the end they offered their home for final conference between the Pequot chief and Miantonomo's brother, Pessicus.

At that time stern terms of submission were laid down. So few Pequot warriors remained alive, so many of their allies had been killed or captured, that awe of English fighting methods spread to every tribe. Peace at last! A sigh of relief swept New England.

End of the Pequot war seemed to mark a new era of expansion. Hundreds of Puritans landed that year. Pioneers were pushing deep into Connecticut and on down the coast. Several of Roger's friends in Salem asked for land in Providence and planned to migrate. Others, like John Greene, a surgeon, who arrived with wife and five children, just appeared and asked to join the householders. Practically every family in the village had cattle now waxing fat on the rich marsh grass. Farms prospered. New houses were going up.

Citizens kept hearing, however, that the older Colonies regarded the settlement on the Moshassuck River as anything but an orderly group. They felt it couldn't be that without more control from magistrate and minister. A single incident brought sharply home to everyone the fear of Providence innovations which haunted authorities in Massachusetts Bay.

In July 1637 John Greene went to Salem on business. A friend whom he met on the village street asked, "How is it with you, Mr. Greene, on Narragansett Bay? Do you not regret leaving Salem?"

"Not I!" replied the visitor warmly. "I could not live in Salem. For here the power of the Lord Jesus is in the hands of civil magistrates."

At this a passer-by whirled around to show the glowering face of John Endicott. "How dare you utter such blasphemy!" roared Salem's leader.

"Is it not true, Mr. Endicott?" retorted Greene, quite unafraid. "In this town a magistrate can punish a man for beliefs different in any way from those laid down by the synod of ministers."

But Endicott was livid with rage and incapable of reasoning. Within an hour he had sent constables to arrest John Greene. A fine of twenty pounds was imposed upon him and he was jailed until the fine was paid.

When a trader from Massachusetts brought Roger this news, he sent letters of strong protest to Endicott and other Salem authorities. But Greene only escaped jail and fine by a trick. He made a statement of submission which he promptly took back the moment he was outside the Colony.

Stirred by this episode, Roger decided that it was high time the citizens of Providence had a clear idea of the kind of government the proprietor had been planning. One summer afternoon all the landowners met on the scythed-down grass in front of the leader's house and placed themselves on the benches set out there. Facing this assembly, Roger experienced a deep inner excitement. A dream was coming true. Here and now in this bit of cleared wilderness an association of free men was forming.

In his belted black tunic, the leader suggested the young minister of Essex rather than a pioneer woodsman. His whole manner indicated an occasion of grave importance.

"Friends," he began, "we are met to consider further how best to govern ourselves in loving peace. To that end I have drawn up a covenant, which, if it be consented to by the majority, we shall sign and shall require to sign all who may come afterwards to live amongst us."

Slowly he unfolded a paper he had brought and read the agreement which, for all its simplicity, represented years of study, thought, keen observation, and painful experience.

*"We, whose names are hereunder written,
being desirous to inhabit in ye town of Providence, do promise to subject ourselves in active
or passive obedience to all such orders or agreements as shall be made (for public good of
our body in an orderly way) by the major
consent of the present inhabitants, masters of
families, incorporated together into a town fellowship and such others whom they shall
admit unto them,*
only in civil things."

There was a long silence. Serious eyes considered the leader
and heads nodded solemnly. Those pioneers had no realization
of sharing in a great event. Yet such it was. Never before in
the history of the human race had a group of people of their
own free will drawn up a contract to live together under government. No king nor powerful proprietor, no commercial company,
no religious body, stood behind this new society. Its own members had full power to frame laws and abide by them. The Providence covenant was an arrow pointing straight to the Declara-
tion of Independence and the Bill of Rights.

At last the hush was broken. John Greene said, "Sirs, did ye
note that by this we do agree 'only in civil things'? The meaning
is plain. Nought commands a man's private belief. Officers we
choose cannot interfere with anyone's way of worship."

"Aye," echoed John Smith. " 'Tis in the way of liberty of conscience that we set a new example here."

Presently William Harris closed the discussion by rasping out,

"There seems nought in this covenant to hold a man down beyond good reason. Let us each sign forthwith."

That evening there was a fine, warm feeling in Roger's heart. It beat to the triumphant words, "A new thing has begun!"

Later, people said that never had he "prophesied" better than at the candle-lighted service held at his house. People met there several times a week to hear him and to read the Bible and discuss religion.

Early in the autumn, Richard Scott and his wife Catherine joined the group. Catherine was the sister of Anne Hutchinson, that much-talked-of woman who was stirring Boston into furious factions. Mrs. Scott herself was a Baptist. Her gentle presentation of faith moved Roger Williams greatly, and he declared that were he to join any church again, it would be that of the Baptists.

Very different in temper was another family group which took land in Providence about this time. A man named William Arnold, his full-grown son, Benedict, his son-in-law, William Carpenter, and their wives and children, built houses on the tract along the river. With some uneasiness the proprietor observed that the man they chose as friend was the surly, discontented William Harris. These men were always pressing a demand for deeds to their ten-acre lots. They were assured that deeds would be made out in due time. Roger was re-establishing his Indian trade, arranging for transport on Dutch ships of his furs and for delivery of merchandise. His every moment was packed with activity.

October twelfth was the date the Massachusetts Bay Company had set for celebrating the Pequot victory and general peace. Many of Roger's friends in the Bay Colony and practically everyone in Providence were aghast to think that he was completely left out of the ceremony. He was not invited to be present and the Council had sent him no letter of thanks for keeping the Narragansetts out of the Pequot league. Whatever his services, he was still the banished heretic, unworthy to step foot on hallowed soil.

That very October afternoon young Benedict Arnold spoke of this injustice. He had gone with Roger out to meet a Dutch sloop which had anchored at the mouth of the river. By this time the trader had met a great many Dutch captains and merchants and was picking up their language with his usual facility. On the way back from the ship Benedict was full of talk.

"It seems, Mr. Williams, that many are displeasured because you be not in Boston for the honors this day. Mayhap if Mr. Harry Vane had not sailed back to England, the invitation would have come for you."

"Nay," said Roger, smiling, "he had more friends among the people than among those in high places."

Benedict pulled on his oars for a ruminative moment. "They say Mistress Hutchinson wept to see him go. She needeth a friend, I'll warrant."

"Aye, lad." Roger's voice was filled with pity. "Likely she will be tried before the General Court. Her husband hath written me about land for a new home."

"Not with us here, Mr. Williams!" Benedict's scowl grew deep. "My father saith 'tis sinful for a woman to preach."

Roger's eyes were following the silver flash of a wild pigeon's wings against the red and gold foliage along the shore. He brought them back to his companion to say gravely, "Every word spoken by Jesus Christ to women reveals He thought their souls as precious as souls of men. Is freedom of conscience to be denied women amongst us, Benedict?"

"Nay, not so," murmured the youth doubtfully.

When they had beached the boat Roger went off at once to take a look at his clam beds. As he came back, he saw young Arnold still engaged in conversation. This time he was talking with John Greene. Suddenly in the autumnal stillness Greene's voice rang out.

"Be not deceived by what you hear from Massachusetts, Benedict. They know the truth there—that Mr. Roger Williams is the man of greatest power in all New England. A thinker and scholar of learning is he, and a good trader and influential with the Indians. Massachusetts fears him, for he is now a great land-owner, doubtless the greatest of any in these parts."

In utter astonishment Roger heard these words. He sank down upon a rock near the path to look for a moment at his own reflection mirrored in his friend's comment. "A great land-owner!" he murmured to himself. Of course it was true. But for his largest holdings he already had a project which would bring a cherished plan one step nearer realization. It was part of an experiment destined to influence two continents.

10

THANK Heaven you are here, Mr. Williams!"
Out of the twilight Thomas James stepped from shore
to a flat rock and seized the canoe's prow. With a powerful shove he drove the craft up the beach and held out a hand
to help lift the trader's heavy pack. James was one of the distinguished newcomers in New Providence, a minister of a church
in Charlestown who had fled from theocratic interference.

Shipping his paddles, Roger said with a smile in his voice,
"What awaits my return this time, friend?"

"Several men and women just arrived here," was the answer.
"Six by boat and three afoot along the trails. They wish to purchase land here and join us. In your three days' absence they have
grown anxious. Will you see them tonight?"

Roger had been knotting the canoe's rope about a gnarled
cedar. "Tonight?" he echoed wearily, then in haste added, "Aye,
Mr. James. Give me half an hour at home, then send them to me."

Heaving up his pack, he strode along the path. At its end he
could see a candle shining through the oiled paper which served
for glass in the window frame. The sight always gave him a
thrill of happiness.

After Mary's warm welcome, he climbed swiftly to the sleeping room for a look at the little girls. Then at the end of the
table near the fire he sat down to a good hot supper. Yet it was

rest more than food for which he longed. For three days he had been paddling, walking through the forest, and holding long sessions with the Indians. Now he wanted to relax. Instead, he had to take down his maps and ledgers from the shelf and begin to work out the plots which could be offered the newcomers. He was still figuring when he heard the expected knock at the door.

Residents of Providence in presenting strangers to the proprietor often had the air of proud showmen. "Here he is!" their eyes seemed to say. "The terrible heretic and firebrand you have heard condemned in Boston!"

Newcomers usually showed in some fashion their surprise at finding the famous rebel concerned only with helping them get settled. He asked few questions and none about religious beliefs. But the soft gaze of his eyes seemed to probe each person to the depths.

On this occasion transactions could only be begun. Plots were pointed out and the candidates sent off to consider the matter. Their worthiness to become citizens had also to be weighed by the freemen of the town.

After the group departed, Thomas James lingered a moment. "Had you news from England in the letters brought down last week?"

Roger motioned his visitor to a seat. "One item of interest. It seems that the two Lords owning the land governed by young Mr. Winthrop were put off coming to America by Mr. Cotton's account of things. When they learned that the church was supreme in all civil matters and tolerated none but its own doctrine and that only church members could vote, they cared not to venture here."

The minister nodded. "Also Mr. Harry Vane's report on Boston's tyranny will make that place no friends. Mayhap our freedom in New Providence is liked better by English Puritans."

Rising to take his leave, James asked, "Is all arranged for Mistress Hutchinson and her family and the other refugees? They are sure now of their lands on Aquidneck?"

He referred to the large island lying near the southeastern shore of Narragansett Bay, which was later called Rhode Island. When it was certain that Anne Hutchinson would be banished from Massachusetts, her husband, together with John Clark, a Baptist made unwelcome in the colony, and William Coddington, came to Roger to find land for new homes. He suggested Aquidneck. But before arranging any purchase, he went with Mr. Hutchinson to see Massasoit and make certain the wily sachem would not set up claim to it.

"Aye," he replied to James, "the Narragansett sachems have sold the island to these families. Mr. Coddington acts as their leader."

James shook his head with humorous amazement over his host's unfailing readiness to serve. " 'Twas Coddington who once as a Bay Company officer voted for your banishment. Yet you assist him now when in his turn he would flee the saints."

He held out his hand in farewell and Roger went with him to close the heavy door against the wild March wind.

From the loft Mary's voice called down, "Husband, bank the fire well before you come."

"Aye, Mary, but first I must write a letter."

"Nay, it is too late."

Her protest was in vain. Only at night could Roger find time for the wide correspondence he constantly kept up. He had to answer a letter from his brother in London, containing the bad news that the trustee of their inheritance had robbed them. Indian matters must be reported to each of the Winthrops, and the writer took time to make sorrowful protests against the harsh treatment of Anne Hutchinson.

When at last he laid down his quill, he stood a moment reviewing his crowded schedule. Even with servants and hired helpers the farm required much of his attention—especially when pigs or cattle were bought or sold. Visitors claimed him almost every day. He had to meet with the town officers, show lands to prospective residents, and calm the disputes which often arose in the growing town.

One thing was now settled. He had offered deeds to twelve of the original settlers. Before he could do so, he had drawn up a paper specifying the boundaries of the grant. Then, after checking it carefully with Canonicus and Miantonomo, he had them sign it before a witness. The mark of Canonicus was a bow, that of his princely nephew was an arrow. This was the first official paper recording the founding of Providence.

Several of Roger's friends had now arrived from Salem. John Throckmorton, Stukeley Westcott, and Richard Waterman were already plastering up the big center chimneys of their almost finished houses. With them had come a man of considerable education and means named Thomas Olney. His house plan boasted of two rooms downstairs. Olney had so impressed his fellow citizens that they elected him treasurer of the town. But he inspired Roger with no sense of trust.

Providence was soon all agog over the Aquidneck settlers. Between their trips to the island where they had started building, they met in Providence to form what they called a Bodie Politik. William Coddington, a man whose carefully curled hair, elegant clothes and haughty manner made him seem more courtier than pioneer, was chosen chief magistrate or judge. When Mr. Hutchinson described the government to Roger, it seemed to him to have a curious likeness to the theocracy from which the organizers had fled. He did not believe the liberal thinkers in the group would tolerate it long.

One noon in late March, Roger came back from shooting a wild turkey to find his fire room filled with people. His eyes went straight to a tall, blonde woman huddled in the armchair against her flung-back cloak. Her pale face drooped with weariness, but at his entrance it lifted and brightened.

"Mistress Hutchinson," he cried, hurrying toward her, "welcome to you."

He was struck by her vibrant handclasp. In the first of his many talks with this vital woman he discovered that she had suffered deeply over the break with John Cotton. It was her admiration for the eloquent preacher of St. Botolph in England which had drawn her to America. For a long time after she had settled in Boston, Cotton had praised her explanations of his sermons to those who met at her house. But, faced with the antagonism of the Elders, he began to withdraw his approval and at her trial had renounced agreement with her doctrine.

"Ah," cried Roger scornfully, "I fear Mr. Cotton betrays his own natural sweetness and now swims with the tide of outward credit and profit."

But a still more bitter disappointment saddened this fearless woman. He discovered it one day when he had paddled over to Aquidneck with supplies and letters brought from Boston by a trader for the new settlers. Roger had looked over the nearly finished house and made suggestions about the garden. Then Anne brought him indoors to have a cup of tea.

Suddenly she leaned forward. "Mr. Harry Vane often spoke of you, Mr. Williams. He said you had taught him much about sound government."

The handsome face of the young man arose before Roger. "That excellent and godly soul will lead the Puritans of England some day. Of that I am certain."

"But we need him here!" Anne's voice had an anguished note. "He alone understood the pinched and evil ways of the Court and magistrates and Elders. He could give hope and courage. If he return not, I would go back to England from this wilderness!"

Amazed by her outburst, Roger weighed it in silence. Better than anyone he could realize this woman's loneliness and disillusion. Now in this untamed spot she must start life again with few special friends or followers. She had already expressed disagreement with John Clark. He was an earnest Baptist and a strong follower of William Coddington. Yet for his part, Roger enjoyed talking with him.

On one of his visits to the island Roger found himself defending to Clark his ideas of democratic government. "Civil magistrates were never appointed by God to be defenders of Christian faith," he argued. "They can have no more power than the people entrust them with."

"But who then leads the people?" asked Clark heatedly. "At

least we Baptists mean to found a church for guide and discipline. In your town there is no church of any sort."

"True," said Roger mildly, "yet there is much seeking after God. Many gather at my house and doubtless at houses of others."

Anne Hutchinson, in whose house the talk was started, looked at the visitor searchingly. "My sister, Mrs. Scott, told me you were almost ready to call yourself a Baptist shortly ago," said she.

But it was not a definite creed Roger wanted. It was experience of the spirit. "We might call ourselves Seekers," he explained. "We meet to share revelations of God. Only those come who so will. There is no compulsion upon any."

Yet compulsion to prevent attendance at these meetings was equally intolerable. Joshua Verin's wife was suddenly and violently stopped from coming by her husband. Roger brought the matter before the town meeting. Verin had said that he saw no sense in such religious conversations and didn't propose to have his wife waste time upon them.

"On liberty of conscience for all doth this town stand," declared Roger Williams vehemently. "For Mr. Verin to abuse his wife for her beliefs is persecution. It must not go unpunished."

Several men uttered entire agreement. Then William Harris spoke. "Sirs," said he with a wicked smile lighting his gnarled features, "it would appear that Mr. Verin doth but follow his own conscience in forbidding his wife to follow hers. To reprove him shows want of principle."

A burst of laughter greeted this sally. But for all their enjoyment of the satire, the freemen of Providence voted to suspend Verin's citizenship until he let his wife pursue her soul's good in peace. Joshua was too stubborn to comply. Promptly he packed up his goods and departed for Salem where the independence of women was disregarded.

It often seemed to Roger that life was one ceaseless debate. He never stepped into the Narragansett country to carry on trade without being harangued by Canonicus. The old sachem was full of discontent because the terms of settlement for the Pequot War had never been met. For this he blamed the English and the tribe they chose to favor, the Mohegans. Mohegan aid had helped win the war. But they had kept an unfair portion of booty and prisoners. Worst of all, they were protecting the murderers of the Block Island trader who brought on the conflict.

With a few congenial spirits gathered about his own fireside, Roger could be frank about this impasse. "The heart of the trouble is that Uncas, sachem of the Mohegans, is protected by authorities in Connecticut. Nor can I think they are ignorant of the wiles and deceits of that tricky heathen."

"Well said, Mr. Williams!" The speaker was a distinguished clergyman and old resident of Massachusetts who had recently settled in Providence. "I know the will of both Connecticut and Massachusetts. It is fixed on possession of all this land at Narragansett Bay. Any move which provides a reason to interfere with us is justified in their eyes. To promote a quarrel between Uncas and the Narragansett tribe might serve. Doubtless Canonicus knows that."

"What evil plotting!" exploded Thomas James. "They chose Mr. Williams as agent, yet give him no support!"

Suddenly a strange episode gave the agent new prestige in all the region. One evening four young men from Plymouth knocked at Roger's door. Learning they were on their way to Aquidneck,

Roger invited them to stay for the night. He was too busy to converse with them that night, and next morning as soon as he had arranged to have them ferried across the bay they hurried off.

It was sunrise then, and as usual Roger began hoeing in his cornfield. Hardly had he started when John Greene, with the skirts of his tunic flying, came leaping over the green rows.

"Come at once!" he called. "A murder has been done. On the trail a Narragansett messenger has been found wounded unto death and robbed to boot!"

In the next hour Roger acted the roles of detective, first-aid worker, and sheriff all at once. With John Greene, to serve as surgeon, and several others, he hurried north to the Pequot trail through the woods. They found the wounded man guarded by Benedict Arnold, who had discovered him first. Greene's effort to staunch the flowing blood had hardly begun when the death rattle sounded in the Indian's throat.

Benedict looked hard at Roger. "It seems, Mr. Williams, that you entertained the murderers of this man. While he still could speak, he told me that four young men coming down the trail from the Plymouth way had fallen upon him here."

Swift action followed this report. A party was hurried into boats for Aquidneck to arrest the four culprits. Then a trusty messenger set off for Boston with a letter from Roger to John Winthrop, reporting the foul deed and asking where trial of the criminals had best take place. Before long Canonicus sent a message demanding vengeance.

Several days passed without answer from Winthrop. The four prisoners were held at the Aquidneck village. After receiving another urgent message from Canonicus, Roger with two Provi-

dence men set off to his house.

The sachem was in a fine state of rage against the English. He had no faith that murder of the messenger would be punished. Look at the way the treachery of Uncas was allowed to continue! Now he—Canonicus—was warning all and sundry through Roger Williams, interpreter and agent, that he meant to wait no longer. He would battle it out with Uncas without more delay.

When his listener begged him to have patience, the eyes of Canonicus smoldered with ire. Picking up a stick beneath the towering fir tree under which they were sitting, he broke it into ten even pieces. These he laid side by side in front of the emissary.

"See!" he growled. "Such are the many lies told to the Narragansetts by English."

Every chieftain in the circle sat tense and silent. It was plain that they only awaited a signal to beat the war drums. Then Roger was on his feet, his mind made up.

"Great Sachem, you have right on your side. I cannot deny the faults of my white brothers. Let us not wait for their decision. Let us go together to Mohegan camp and command Uncas to obey the treaty terms."

Each swarthy face lifted in exultation. Miantonomo raised his arms above his head in a gesture of thankfulness. Immediately plans were made to start next day for the Connecticut Valley.

At dawn began the strange procession. With his wife and children and several lesser chieftains, Miantonomo led the way. Roger and his two companions from Providence followed. On either side walked an armed guard of some two hundred and fifty braves. When night fell, fires were lighted for protection. The princess and her children lay close together, wrapped in otter skins. Outside the ring of fires sentinels paced the night through. For hours of the first night's camp Roger could not sleep for savoring the primitive scene. Only the plash of a distant waterfall, the hoot of an owl, and the sharp bark of a fox on a distant hill pricked the stillness. Firelight wavered softly over the motionless forms of sleeping warriors. When the plumy crest of the pine trees shifted, a star glittered far aloft.

After three days they reached the village of the Mohegan chief. With every appearance of good faith the visitors were welcomed. But, for all his observance of diplomatic courtesy, Roger made it plain to Uncas from the first that a just settlement was to be made then and there. No more evasions nor delays!

Without spoken protest Uncas accepted Miantonomo's four-point pact. The Pequot murderers were to be executed. The remainder of the tribe was to be divided between Narragansetts and Mohegans. Uncas and Miantonomo promised to do one another no further injury. Finally, both pledged themselves to accept English mediation of future disagreements.

Completely satisfied, Miantonomo said gratefully to Roger, "This better than war and killing. Once more my friend spoke truly and acted with wisdom."

Leaving the Narragansetts to their ceremonies of peace, Roger sped home over the trails. At last John Winthrop had written that the trial of the four prisoners should be held at Plymouth. At once Roger started for the town with the culprits, their guards, and both Indian and English witnesses. Before the trial took place one prisoner escaped. But the others confessed their guilt and were hanged in the presence of Indian representatives.

Swiftly over the region ran the news to all the tribes that a crime against an Indian had been swiftly punished. Massasoit, Canonicus, and many another sachem sent word that the trial had restored faith in English justice and good faith. At Providence Roger was received like a conquering hero.

Any gathering of townsfolk these days was of considerable size. The population was periodically increased by families waiting to make homes on Aquidneck where fertile fields and good harbors beckoned. An equally valuable but smaller island had been offered by Canonicus to Williams and the latter persuaded John Winthrop to join him in buying it for raising swine. In addition to Prudence Island, as he called it, Roger bought two other small islands where he started market gardens.

Progress among this handful of pioneers was typical of all the New World. What was known of the vast continent was a mere narrow ribbon of territory along the Atlantic Coast. But so rapidly were ships unloading settlers in harbors north and south that villages were springing up like mushrooms in New England; Virginia plantations were spreading; Lord Baltimore was starting a colony in Maryland; and west of the Hudson River English, Dutch, and Swedes were turning woods into pleasant farms. Every new outpost meant that more sailboats went up and down the coast to exchange produce and farm animals between the Colonies. Therefore each year a certainty grew stronger in the hearts of all transplanted folk. Now they knew they belonged to the strange, untamed country which they had learned to call home.

In late September of 1638 a great happiness came to the Williams family. A son and heir was born. The delighted father, marveling at the small wrinkled being who was to carry on his name, wanted to call him Providence. Mary thought the name seemed to set a seal of joy upon their life in the big log house.

Just before the baby's arrival Roger had taken a step long contemplated by "the great landowner." At a meeting of the freemen on August 8th he presented his plan.

He was giving up his absolute ownership of Providence Plantations. All the lands not already assigned to residents were turned over to a Proprietor's Company. It consisted of twelve men chosen by Roger for their capacity to undertake transfers and management of future lots. Each would be an equal trustee with him and they could outvote him if they wished. His land monopoly was at an end.

The sensation made by this announcement was tremendous. One after another men sprang to their feet with questions.

"Will these twelve men remain without change in their places of power?" demanded William Harris.

" 'Tis no place of power, but of trust alone," was the answer. "A member of the Proprietor's Company has no more rights in the town corporation than other freemen. The company holds in trust all undivided and common lands for sale. It will serve all citizens and those who come to live amongst us. Its duties are the same as mine have been."

William Arnold now arose. "Do these twelve men, Mr. Williams, have the power to say who shall buy land and who not?"

"Nay, Mr. Arnold. The freemen vote on new persons as before. Nought in our town government is changed. A company supplants me as proprietor. That is the whole of it."

For a long moment there was silence. Then Thomas James said in a deep voice, " 'Tis a fine, strange thing—this act of Mr. Williams. Up in Boston members of the Massachusetts Bay Company do by tricks and wiles secure for themselves hundreds of acres to sell or hold. But our leader puts much of his land in charge of others for the good of all."

"Amen to that!" spoke out many voices.

It was late when the session was over. Roger felt happy and excited. As he stepped out of the meeting room, he found the moon flooding over houses and fields and the grassy road they called the Towne Street. It was still thrilling to him to realize that a little over two years ago this was but a wild tract of woods and meadows. Now it was a place where men were making a town, making a government, making America.

John Greene touched his arm gently. With a look of deep curiosity, he said, "My friend, is there any gain to you in this change to a company?"

"Aye, that there is!" Roger gave a deep-throated laugh. "I have associates now to keep the books of land sales and satisfy newcomers to the town. My head is broken with the task."

So pleased was he to share responsibility that in December of that year he organized another land-holding company. He did so partly because the Arnolds and William Harris were always pressing him for more tracts. What he deeded to this group of thirteen individuals, including himself, was the meadow land southwest of Providence on the Pawtuxet River. Each of the thirteen men had an equal share in the monopoly and twelve were to pay Williams an amount which was to total some twenty pounds.

It was with much satisfaction that on the evening of December 31, 1638, Roger sat by the fire reviewing the events of the year just ending. He had divested himself of much arbitrary power associated with being a proprietor. That he had never wanted.

What he was working toward was a self-ruling colony of men firmly rooted upon their own acres. A beginning had been made. He gave a sigh of contentment. Even the storm that rattled the shutters was to his liking.

Turning to Mary, who was dipping candles at the hearth, he said, "This snow is good for our fields, my dear. Our beasts are warm and so are we. 'Tis a night to thank God for our blessings."

He did not know what the storm he praised had brought to Aquidneck. A refugee from Massachusetts and from Plymouth was blown by it into the settlement there. He was given shelter and food and a chance to bring his family and remain. This man, Samuel Gorton, was to prove such a center of quarreling and discontent as to shake the region from end to end. Nevertheless, in the marvelous way that good comes out of evil, Gorton was the exciting cause of great events both in the life of the Colony and in the career of its founder.

11

IT takes time for ferment to work. Samuel Gorton, fermenter in chief of Narragansett Bay, caused bubbles to rise some twelve months after arriving at Aquidneck. But it needed nearly three years to get the whole region boiling.

On a trading trip to the island in the summer of 1639 Roger first met the man. He was an excitable person, small of stature and full of talk. In no time it could be seen that in religion he was a mystic, but in politics he seemed to run the gamut between formalism and anarchy. Anne Hutchinson told Roger on the occasion of his visit that Gorton's ideas helped to combat the autocratic views of William Coddington.

"Mr. Gorton is one of us who object to the proposals recently put forward by our chief magistrate."

Roger was not surprised to learn that Coddington's ambitions were now revealed. He suggested governing the island "by God's rule." He was willing to have three Assistants, but wished the freemen to have only veto power upon his decisions and rulings. John Clark backed the Governor, but the majority of residents refused the proposition. Thereupon Clark and Coddington moved down to the southern part of the island and, with their supporters, founded the village of Newport. The older settlement called itself Portsmouth and the island was renamed Rhode Island.

In 1640, however, the two towns agreed to join under the Governorship of Coddington and to set up a court which would hold quarterly sessions. It was then that Samuel Gorton, refusing to sign the agreement, began to lift up his voice.

"This is no legal government without a charter from King Charles," he repeated. "Neither your lands nor your authority have proper title."

When Williams went to Newport to do business with a Dutch sea captain, he found John Clark seething with fury over the rebel of Portsmouth.

"Look ye, Mr. Williams. Because many of us were ill received in Massachusetts we took pity on Mr. Gorton after he was banished out of Plymouth. But we also may have to exile him—albeit for a most different reason than had Governor Bradford."

"I have heard that reason." Roger's eyes brimmed with amusement. A servant of Gorton's had smiled in church and was hailed into court. For defending her the employer had been exiled from Massachusetts Colony. "His independency is to be admired. Mayhap, however, in your midst at Rhode Island he doth show it forth too strongly."

"Aye, indeed!" snorted Clark. "Mr. Gorton declares he is as fit and able to govern himself and his family as any on the island and will submit to no rulings. He stirs up many against the Court. Not long, Mr. Williams, can we tolerate this person."

That autumn the threat of exile was carried out. Naturally Samuel Gorton sought refuge in New Providence. With him came a number of persons devoted to his religious and social ideas, and before he had been in the village a week he had gathered about him many more followers.

Caution bade Roger advise delay in granting the newcomer

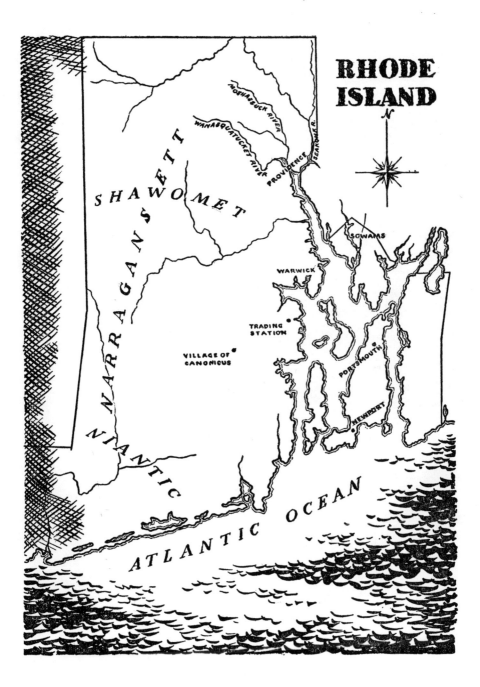

citizenship. To the town council and to the Proprietor's Company alike he said, "Let Mr. Gorton first prove that he will abide by the laws of our corporate body."

These laws had recently been revised. A committee of four had worked out twelve articles as a primitive constitution and thirty-nine freemen had signed them. Liberty of conscience was formally adopted as a principle. Each landowner was to receive a deed for his property and disputes about land or other matters were to be settled by arbitration. Another committee was given the task of drawing a proper line between the boundaries of Providence and the meadow lands of the Pawtuxet tract possessed by the thirteen owners. In the light of such accomplishment, Gorton's harping criticism of the government was particularly unwelcome.

"Mr. Gorton bemaddens this poor town," Roger said at a council meeting, "but let us have patience till this strong spirit finds its way amongst us."

Far greater was his own anxiety over Indian unrest. Uncas had still failed to live up to his agreement made at Hartford, and the Narragansetts knew perfectly well his defiance was based on the connivance of the Connecticut authorities.

As Roger paddled up the wild rivers or stalked through the forest on the way to Indian camps, he suffered an aching loneliness. Banished and impeded by the powerful men of New England, he had to depend on his own efforts alone to overcome tribal suspicion by truth and justice. Why could Englishmen not trust him as did the savages?

Returning from one of these long trips in the summer of 1641, he found Providence in turmoil. As he stepped out of his canoe, an uproar on Towne Street brought him rushing up the bank. A dozen men were fighting like tigers. But at that moment several of them broke away and tore off toward the meadows with the others in hot pursuit. Plunging after them through the long grass, Roger heard the sound of a gun.

On the scene of battle, he swiftly wrested from one reckless hand a brandished pitchfork and shouted that the fighting must stop. Meanwhile other townsmen were helping pull the antagonists apart.

When the hubbub had calmed down and the wounded had limped home to be bandaged by their wives, Roger was told what caused the outbreak. One of Gorton's followers, doubtless misunderstanding the leader's radical teachings, had refused to pay a just debt. When, with the legal sanction of the town court, an attempt was made to take the man's cow in payment, he and other Gortonists resisted forcibly.

At an indignation meeting of the citizens, Roger said, "What is gravest about this affair is the division here amongst us. Everyone takes sides. That makes a quarrel hard to mend."

Although he finally patched up that dispute, Roger could not establish harmony. Three parties divided the town into Gortonists, loyalists to the Providence government, and dissenters who made their insistence on Gorton's banishment an excuse for destructive criticism. Worse followed. The latter party, led by William Harris and William Arnold, together with his son Benedict, took a step which threatened the very existence of the settlement. These men and their friends and relatives appealed to the Massachusetts General Court to accept them under its authority.

That action turned the village into a hive of angry bees. Every night people would gather in the Williams house to ask, "How dare they?" "What does it mean?" Roger frankly told the questioners that he believed greed for land had made certain individuals actual enemies of their society. In sore disgust and passionate anxiety he waited for the answer to the outrageous appeal.

When it came, a sigh of relief swept the supporters of the 1640 compact. The General Court refused to take any action unless all Providence submitted entirely either to Plymouth or to Massachusetts. A stormy town meeting made it plain that the majority of residents scorned the suggestion.

Samuel Gorton solved his own problem by moving his family and a number of followers into the tract along the Pawtuxet River. But that was the very section which Harris and the Arnolds wanted to absorb. Without severing themselves formally from Providence, they followed Gorton, took up land along the Pawtuxet and began to build houses. Part of the acreage they used lay outside the original grant to Roger Williams. The Narragansetts objected, and it required both Roger's diplomacy and contributions from his own purse to satisfy the sachems. From the moment Harris and Arnold went to Pawtuxet, they began to use every possible means to drive Gorton out of the district.

First they went up to Boston and placed themselves and their new lands under the jurisdiction of the General Court. Next, they persuaded the Shawomets, a tribe of Indians subordinate to the Narragansetts, to do likewise. The chiefs hoped by that obeisance to the white rulers to shake off the yoke of their masters. Arnold and Harris set about persuading the General Court that Samuel Gorton had no right to be at Shawomet and should be forced out for heresy, anarchy, and disturbance of the peace.

Such tactics had caused Roger to feel great pity for Gorton.

Time after time he went down to Shawomet to reason with his enemies and try to establish friendly relations. One afternoon as he came back to town the fatigue and worry on his face startled a passer-by. He was Chad Brown, three years a resident, and now one of Roger's most trusted friends.

"You are tossed about by this Pawtuxet affair, Mr. Williams!" Brown cried in concern. "Stop at my fireside a moment for rest and a cool glass of ale."

When he had placed his guest on the high-backed settle, glass in hand, Brown sat across the hearth. "'Tis no easy matter to start a settlement in freedom," he said in a gloomy tone. "Many of us wonder you do not lose heart here. Enemies at home and abroad working against us!"

Already Roger looked relaxed and able to smile at the human comedy. "With men of force, the like of whom drift here, things cannot be smooth. Those men of Pawtuxet are selfish and unruly. Yet even they signed that clause in our compact which provides for liberty of conscience. 'Tis progress so far."

"If only this appeal for domination by the Bay Company doth not encourage it to take measures against us. They seek cause to do so!"

Chad Brown's opinion was echoed by Anne Hutchinson. She had heard from friends that the General Court censored the liberal measures taken by Rhode Island citizens that year. Eight magistrates were now elected by majority vote and Coddington's power was less arbitrary. The fact drew down abuse from Massachusetts.

Roger tried to allay the fears of Mrs. Hutchinson. Yet his own lonely hours were filled with doubts. The whole effort to found a democratic state, freed from the church, might fail! It could go down in a welter of personal hatreds. If it did, here was something more than a local defeat. For what happened in this tiny village on America's coast was linked with that great campaign for liberty which had been launched only recently overseas. England—his own England—was at last in open revolt against tyranny.

News of this revolt kept coming to the Colonies. It had all started with the Scotch Presbyterians. When they openly defied King Charles and his minion, Archbishop Laud, the arrogant monarch resolved to send an army against them. But in order to pay that army, he was obliged to summon Parliament to vote him grants. In April 1640 representatives of the nation met for the first time in eleven years.

A determined set of men! They wouldn't even listen to royal demands for money until they had drawn up a long list of grievances. In a fury they were dismissed.

London, however, was rising against oppression. The populace made such a scene before the Archbishop's palace that Laud had had to flee. Merchants and citizens of every religious view joined in backing Parliament. Meanwhile the Scotch, refusing to yield an inch, were training an army.

Eagerly Williams waited for each ship from England. What was happening now? Were opposers to absolute power able to hold their own? At last in the summer of 1642 he found within a packet brought down from Boston one letter from London. As he caught sight of it, he called out to his wife. She must come listen to this. It was from Mr. Harry Vane.

In a voice tense with excitement he read her at once the great news. In November 1640 Parliament had reassembled. This time the stoutest champions of English liberty resolved to sit the struggle out. Their stubbornness resulted in a session which has ever since been called the Long Parliament.

Smoldering Cromwell; mighty Pym; dauntless Hampden, now a national hero because he had refused to pay the illegal tax called ship-money which the King had tried to raise; Oliver St. John, husband of Lady Masham's daughter, Jug, the brilliant lawyer who had ably defended Hampden at his trial; John Selden—these were only a few of the names which made the Long Parliament a roll of honor. As Roger read Vane's letter, all his acquaintances of other years rose before him and he felt he could almost hear the eloquent words which the stained glass windows and rich carvings of St. Stephen's Chapel must be echoing. That stately room where the Commons sat was now a battleground for the rights of Englishmen.

Of course, Vane himself was in the thick of the fray. He was one of a group working to abolish the infamous Star Chamber. Already its victims had been released from the Tower to walk, free men, between cheering London crowds. Vane was also adding his voice to the chorus which cried for the impeachment of Archbishop Laud. When that happened, Parliament would go even further. It meant to remove forever the political power of bishops.

As he slowly folded up the letter, Mary remarked, "So? Mr. Vane is now Sir Harry Vane, isn't he!"

Roger looked startled. He had hardly been aware of this personal item in his friend's news. Then, with a little smile, he pinched his wife's cheek. "Wilt thou like him better, my dear, because of his title?" he said teasingly. Then his face changed. For a moment he stared at her with eyes which had never before glowed with such joy.

"Mary," said he, "do you know how long I have been waiting for this hour to strike in England? For twenty-three years—ever since as a lad I first stepped into the Star Chamber to take shorthand notes for Sir Edward Coke."

More news was soon exchanged between those Providence citizens who had served as lawyers or ministers in London. One of them learned from a brother that Parliament was raising an army to protect itself against King Charles. Another brought word that Archbishop Laud was in prison and that his colleague, commander of Ireland, had been executed. Both King and Parliament were trying to win Scottish support. Plots and counterplots followed hard upon one another.

John Winthrop wrote Roger that few passengers landed these days. Instead, Puritan leaders in England wanted key men to come over from America. Hugh Peters was returning. He was going to represent Massachusetts in London. The struggle there had reached such a height that it was hard to get any attention for the affairs of New England.

Thomas James came to Roger one morning with an offer to help him row over to Rhode Island. He had just learned of a momentous English event which he wanted to discuss on the way. Parliament had forced the King to sign a bill which made it impossible for that body to be dismissed without its own consent. The two men marveled that such a measure could have passed.

"Even Sir Edward Coke went not that far," said Roger. " 'Tis as much as to say that Parliament could rule without the Crown."

James stopped paddling a moment to reflect. "Mayhap reform goes too far and His Majesty not far enough. The old system called the Crown in Parliament is best for England."

Roger thought of the many times debate had been stopped by Charles and the number of patriots who had been flung into the Tower. "Both King James and his son Charles came to look upon Parliament only as a tool for their absolute power. This struggle had to be!"

As 1642 drew on, fewer vessels landed from England and news grew scarce. The colonists began to feel cut off from the motherland. Roger Williams was disturbed by the possibility that Massachusetts and Plymouth might take advantage of that isolation to extend their claims over Narragansett Bay. Presently rumors confirmed his fears.

Rhode Island settlers became uneasy. William Coddington was nervous about his estates and Anne Hutchinson feared for her personal freedom. The recent death of her husband left her more alone than ever. The Elders of the Boston Church had sent men to question her activities. She made up her mind to leave the island before some excuse for taking her before the General Court had been discovered. Through Governor Kieft of New Amsterdam she bought land owned by the Dutch on Pelham Bay and made plans to move her family there.

Sorrowfully Roger went to Portsmouth to bid her farewell. Her influence had been on the side of liberal government and he hated to see her go. It was unbearable that this gifted woman should have been so persecuted.

One day in August the threat of interference from the Bay Company sounded loud in Roger's ears. He was mending his sailboat on the beach when Samuel Gorton came striding up.

"I have news, Mr. Williams!" he shouted. "The General Court of Massachusetts has summoned me to appear before it to answer charges. Charges! That is the work of William Harris and that headstrong young fool, Benedict Arnold!"

With folded arms, Roger looked down at the fierce little man. The split he had created in the Colony was now a yawning abyss. Such a summons meant that the New England powers had found a new opening through which to reach for control of Narragansett territory.

"What answer have you made, Mr. Gorton?" Roger's tone was low and tense.

"What answer? Sir, with all the might descending upon me from the Heavenly Host I have refused to go! The Court knoweth well and so do my enemies that it hath no jurisdiction over me. My land lies some twenty miles west of the Bay Company's grant by charter. I am not one to submit to illegal orders!"

Roger could have flung his hat in air. In this issue, at least, the man's stubbornness was a good weapon. "Justice is on your side, Mr. Gorton," he said warmly. "But will this refusal not worsen things for you in Pawtuxet?"

Gorton's small head under his tall black hat nodded in agreement. "Aye. So sure of this am I that I mean to buy land further off, outside the territory of the Pawtuxet Indians. I shall move south on that neck of land called Shawomet from the tribe living there. I have come to ask you to make a treaty with the sachem Canonicus."

Promising to help him, Roger said, "I pray the Spirit's Grace may soften the hearts of your opponents."

A bitter laugh answered him. "They will no more soften than do these gray rocks at touch of foam. 'Tis but the beginning of interference, Mr. Williams, mark my words!"

Soon this opinion was on many lips. Like dry leaves before November gales, rumors came drifting into Providence. Everyone was asking what was afoot and whether the matter boded good or ill.

A project of major significance was shaping in New England. The governments of the four Colonies were going to form a union. These were Plymouth, Massachusetts, the new settlement on the coast called New Haven, and Connecticut. The latter group was a coalition of Hartford, Saybrook, and several other towns in the Connecticut River Valley. The union offered the first faint hint of the dauntless little nation which began its work one hundred and forty-seven years later.

For colonial leaders to exchange mutual jealousies for co-operation meant just one thing. They were afraid. Forced by English upheavals to depend on themselves, they were combining for defense. Since relations between England and Holland had grown unfriendly, the Dutch in America were becoming hostile to Englishmen.

Worse than this threat, however, was the possibility of a general Indian uprising. Between Mohegans and Narragansetts fury was growing white hot. The wild Mohawks and lesser tribes, such as the Niantics, were ready to fan any flame that might destroy the white race. Thanks to white traders, the braves now had many guns and Indian warfare was more dangerous than ever. Down the coast, the Algonquins had risen against the Dutch and wiped out the settlements on Staten Island. Even friendly tribes were restless and suspicious of the muddled and unjust policy of white leaders.

A federation of New England governments was brilliant statesmanship. Each of its four members was to choose two commissioners and, under a president, the eight men would meet once or twice a year to decide questions of general welfare.

To Providence and Rhode Island, however, the plan brought a distinct threat. Those settlements had not been invited to join the others. Far from it. Hints were many that the federation meant to absorb these outcasts and impose upon them the New England pattern of religion and government.

Town meetings in Providence, in Portsmouth, in Newport! Central gatherings of officials from each town and even from Gorton's little group at Shawomet! Differences were forgotten in the sudden fear of losing independence. For the first time men realized the freedom they had enjoyed. To be forced under theocratic rule again was a fear-stirring thought.

At these conferences the one question was, What can we do to resist aggression from the New England Federation? The one answer was, "Unite!" Only by pooling the resources of the four settlements, only by facing the Federation with solidarity of their own could they fend off encroachment. At last it was clear to all. The citizens of Narragansett Bay must form an independent Colony.

But in those days the only way to establish a Colony was by authority from the King. Otherwise it had no legal status. A charter was necessary and from England alone it could be had. Once, however, a patent from the mother country was secured, even a small Colony had standing in the world. Separate settlements might be engulfed by powerful neighbors. But it would be hard to absorb a Colony chartered by the Crown.

Months of debate in assemblies led straight to one decision. A representative must go to London to apply for a charter. At that point argument ceased. All agreed that an experienced, trusted, influential diplomat was needed and that diplomat was Roger Williams.

From the first he had seen this outcome. And he was ready. The project was the very shape of his dream. All he had ever needed for action was the united will of the people. As 1643 began, that will grew even stronger. For the New England Federation had published its common purpose and flaunted its intention to place Maine, Providence, and all of Rhode Island under its control. The Federation also darkly hinted that it was to undertake "enterprises" and "to divide the spoils of whatever is gathered under conquest."

When these plans were reported in Providence, the little group of his intimates hastened to Roger's house. What did such phrases mean, they wanted to know.

Chad Brown asked anxiously, "Will the Federation send armed men against us?"

Roger stared at the crackling chestnut logs. "Likely there might be first a move against the Narragansetts who dominate the region and own the land. Plots have long been afoot. Canonicus has pledged his tribe to start no trouble with the Mohegans. But Connecticut men foment trouble in the hope that promise will be broken."

When time for his departure drew near, Roger went over for a final interview with the Narragansett sachems. He found them sad and anxious for the future. Talk of peace was brittle as glass before their stony silence.

Miantonomo flung back his magnificent head. "Only you speak truth, friend. English forget Narragansett help in Pequot War. Now they love Uncas—snake and teller of many lies. Uncas not keep treaty. Mohegan men kill our braves by stealth. It is known to English, but not punished. My people call for vengeance!"

Who could deny his dilemma? The Narragansetts were trapped between the plots of greedy white men and jealous Indians. To let Uncas pursue his treacherous ways without a fight would reap scorn for the great, powerful tribe from the whole world of Red Men. Yet to attack the Mohegans meant that the United Colonies might come down in force upon the Narragansetts and wipe them out in deadly battle.

With tears in his eyes, Roger placed his hands on Miantonomo's shoulders. "I shall pray for your safety and for love between your people and my people."

But farewell was not permitted to be mournful. First he had to feast with all the sachems and young princes on strawberries and strawberry cake. Then there was an exchange of gifts. Roger had brought a mirror for Miantonomo's wife which delighted everyone. Joking and laughing, Miantonomo and his young sons escorted their visitor to his canoe. Gaily they spoke of the great feast they would prepare when he returned from the land across the ocean. But as Roger took up his paddle and raised his hand in good-by, his heart contracted with an awful premonition that he was looking for the last time upon his friend.

By early summer Roger had his affairs in order. He had a large household to provide for. There were now five children and Mary expected another baby in early winter. The farm was doing well under an intelligent manservant, and supplies would be ample. Mary had a good helper in the house and many friends in the village. She was not uneasy to be left. But often she mourned that no one would keep her in touch with great events or spread over the daily routine the shimmer of exciting ideas.

Roger could not sail from Boston. Massachusetts officials would not permit the exile to cross their borders. He had to be picked up by a coastal vessel and taken to New Amsterdam to wait there for a ship going to England.

"I may be long upon the Island of Manhattoes," he said to Mary. "But I shall send thee word, dear wife, and do thou give some ship captain a message for me about the children and affairs here."

When the moment of parting came, Roger took his wife and children in his arms and committed them to the mercy of God. Escorted by friends and town officers to the shore, he was just about to go aboard the ship waiting for him there when an Indian runner dashed through the crowd to his side.

"Miantonomo puts on war paint," stated the Narragansett gravely. "Mohegan men must die for new evils done."

With this dire news of Miantonomo's broken promise, Roger set off on the first lap of his momentous journey. It was but one of five terrible events happening that late summer and autumn of 1643.

*your
ere be
anfwere
ns yͤ
cíti nto
gon all u
with my vrst
Earnest lyher do braven yͭ rut
yͭ coogͬ vnworthy
Roger Williams*

12

G UEDEN *dag, mijn Heer!"*
"Good day, sirrr!"
The jolly Dutchman who spoke the last greeting
leaned along the forecastle rail to smile triumphantly down at
Roger Williams. Then as if to underscore his newly acquired
English phrase, he flung his hand out to the horizon.

Roger's glance followed the sweep of that plump hand. Limitless was the expanse of smoothly rolling sea, streaked with deep color and electric with sparks of brilliant summer sunlight. Both men nodded and smiled. It was, for a wonder, a very good day.

Evidently the ship's mate thought so, too. From his post on the quarter deck hurtled down a sharp command. It took a moment for Roger to translate the roar into "Hoist the top sail!" Before he was sure of it, there came the clump of wooden shoes below and then the Dutch sailors were climbing into the shrouds. So light a wind demanded that every bit of canvas be spread to hasten the vessel on its way to England.

"What are you writing there, *mijn Heer?*"

Curiously the Dutchman looked down at his fellow passenger. Seated in a sheltered corner of the forecastle, with inkhorn, quill, and a sheaf of papers beside him, Roger had been busy all the shining morning. Now, however, it was the hour when he and this new acquaintance exchanged lessons in Dutch and English. He gathered up his papers and rose to his feet.

"I make a translation of Indian words into English," he replied. "This is a key into the American language, together with some observations on the manners and customs of the savages. I hope to publish the same in London."

"So!" Puzzled blue eyes stared at the manuscript. "You like the murdering heathen enough to make a book about them?"

A shiver ran over the slender man in his black Puritan garb. "Many terrible acts must be laid upon the savages. Yet deeds of darkness, unworthy of Christians, have also been done by white men against the Indians."

Roger had been close to these frightful misdeeds during the strange weeks of waiting for the Dutch ship to sail. Even on the day he landed at New Amsterdam from Providence Indian troubles were upon him.

His first impression of the settlement held several surprises. It was odd after scudding down the channel east of the wild, wooded stretches of Manhattoes to sail into so vast a harbor and find at the island's tip a thriving village. At the water's edge a fort faced the harbor solidly. Roger followed the owner of the boat up the muddy bank toward the houses seen from the water. Then he discovered that in addition to the fort itself the high stockade enclosed the barracks, a large building, a church, and a considerable tract of ground. Sentries at the gate gave the place the air of an armed camp.

"That house next the fort is where the Governor lives," explained Roger's companion.

In strong contrast was the peaceful look of the village beyond. A circle of log huts was widely spaced beyond an open green. Among them were several well-finished structures with high, thatched roofs and latticed windows. Many little garden plots offered bright splotches of color. Rosy-cheeked women in kirtles of red and blue were working in their vineyards, and a group of men gathered on the green were smoking long-stemmed pipes. The unexpected gaiety of the scene charmed the Puritan from Providence.

Cheerfulness was only on the surface of New Amsterdam, however. Roger was at once met with fearful tales of killings and burnings by Indians. The Algonquin tribe was on the warpath. Many settlers on both sides of the Hudson River had been massacred and everyone was afraid. Within an hour after his arrival Roger was sent for by Governor Kieft. The Englishman's reputation as ambassador to the Indians had gone before him and the worried official wished his help in making peace.

Roger well knew that many of the Dutch traders had cheated

the Indians right and left. The Governor admitted that they had also sold rum and arms to the natives. Moreover, Roger's questions drew out the fact that neither the Governor himself nor the rich landowners, called patroons, had ever made much effort to win the friendship of Algonquin chiefs. Indeed in February Kieft had attacked the Indians in a bloody raid. There was, consequently, small hope of working out a lasting treaty. But the friend of Indians went with Governor Kieft to meet the sachems.

Then an old story was repeated. In the name of their gods and of the Christian Lord, Roger spoke of peace and good will. His loving words of fellowship astonished the Algonquins. Never had they met such a white man. He soothed their wounded feelings, wrung apologies and promises from both the Governor and the sachems, and patched up an agreement which ended the war for the moment. In New Amsterdam the peacemaker was hailed as a savior.

During the long voyage Roger thought deeply about the difficult problems of human society. How could men learn to combine personal freedom with protection of common rights and also with the mutual effort necessary for trade? Were they going to work out a plan in England?

At New Amsterdam he had had late news of English affairs. More than a year before, Parliament had despaired of restoring the balance of power between the Crown and representatives of the people. Several acts of violence against members of the House of Commons had been plotted by the King. Each one was discovered and foiled. But each carried the nation further toward civil war. At last King Charles resolved to fight for his absolute power. He set up his standard and gradually the royalists flocked

to support him. Battles had occurred. Charles was strongly en-
camped at Oxford. London, all on the side of Parliament, was
preparing defenses. But what had happened since spring of this
year of 1643 was still to be discovered.

In a mood of tremendous excitement Roger entered London
for the first time in eleven years. As he sniffed the hot summer
air, he seemed to breathe in a mood of suspense. The city's em-
battled state was marked by the presence of soldiers everywhere.
They were dressed like other citizens except that they carried
muskets and wore scarves of orange, the colors of Lord Essex,
head of the Parliamentary army. Cannon were implanted at the
gates of the old city wall and before them sentries marched up
and down. A year ago the Cavaliers, as Royalists were contemptuously called, had nearly taken the city, and threat of their doing
so hung over it always.

Securing lodgings near St. Martins in the Fields, the returned
native set out at once for Westminster. Had the streets always
been so noisy, he wondered? Used as he was to the silence of
forest and wild rivers and to the small sounds of pioneer villages, he found the din unbelievable. It was strange also for a
man who knew everyone around Narragansett Bay to find amid
the passers-by not a single familiar face.

But the moment he entered Westminster Hall he saw someone he recognized. "Mr. Oliver St. John!" he cried warmly.
"Well met after long absence across the seas!"

St. John looked his amazement. When he learned who was
greeting him, an expression of eager curiosity spread over his
clever face. His look clouded at Roger's inquiries about Mrs. St.
John, the lovable Jug, and about her mother and stepfather, the

Mashams. Jug had died two years before, but her parents were in good health.

Then St. John said imperiously, "Mr. Williams, if you have not dined, repair with me now to the Royal Arms Tavern. It is quite close by. There we can talk. I do crave direct word about the New England Colonies."

It was astonishing to the pioneer from the wilderness to find himself once more in a crowded tavern. There was a sort of inn at Salem, but he had never crossed its threshold. Seated at a table opposite the handsomely dressed gentleman, now Solicitor General for the realm, Roger made the most of the occasion. After giving his companion a bird's-eye view of American affairs, he pressed St. John for a sketch of England's situation.

"It is grave," replied the official with a frown. "Hope of betterment is fixed on Oliver Cromwell who commands a well-chosen body of troops and trains them strictly. He wrote me that he had a 'lovely company' and they are known as Ironsides."

His listener's dark eyes glowed. "A man of power, I remember."

"Aye. Would there were more like him. Alas, our Chief Captain has just been defeated and the town of Bristol is hard besieged. Lord Essex delays too much. In June, because he would not swiftly bring up his troops against the King's forces, John Hampden—always at the forefront of action and the one who saved the day at Edgehill—was surrounded and slain!"

"Hampden slain!" Roger paled with shock. The loss of so noble a champion of liberty threw a livid light on the terrible cost of civil war.

There were other serious losses in the liberal group. Many of the Puritan nobles had been killed in battle. For most of the new recruits and volunteers—Roundheads, they were called—were as yet no match for the Cavaliers.

"Doth Mr. John Pym still rule the House of Commons?" asked Roger.

St. John smiled, "The word is well chosen. He is called King Pym and his rule is good. His was the plan for the Grand Remonstrance, printed and sent about the whole land, which faced King Charles with all the evils of his reign. Pym was also persuasive to the Scotch and more than anyone he hath set going the great synod for church reform representing all England."

St. John meant the Westminster Assembly, meeting in the Henry Seventh Chapel of Westminster Abbey. It consisted of two ministers from every county and thirty laymen from Parliament, of whom St. John himself was one.

"You will meet many of the divines, Mr. Williams," said he, "and will find amongst us all division of opinion—especially in the matter of church government."

He added that agreement was general on doctrine and form of service. For the vast majority were against Episcopacy as it had been practiced under Archbishop Laud. Remembering vaguely that Roger had been opposed to any sort of national church, St. John asked him what name he gave his faith.

Roger had no desire to discuss his views with this young worldling. Politely replying that he was a Seeker, one who searches for the inner light of truth, he turned the subject to Sir Harry Vane. Vane, he was told, was in Scotland on the important business of promoting union of that people with the Parliamentary group. The Scots had declared they would send their army across the border to fight King Charles on two conditions. The English must help the Scotch Parliament and also accept unity of religion for the two countries.

"A wonderful head hath Sir Harry on those young shoulders," said St. John warmly. "And now at last he hath the sanction and friendship of his father who could no longer support His Majesty."

As the two men rose to go, the Solicitor said, "Since Mr. Hugh Peters from Salem hath been in London, there is much talk of placing your plantations on Narragansett Bay under the sway of Massachusetts. But Sir Harry Vane opposes this. Nothing is decided. You are not too late. For a new Commission must be appointed to deal with all the Colonies."

To digest this mass of information Roger walked slowly along the Thames in the direction of St. Paul's. It was fascinating to see the spires and towers rise up again, to watch the boats on the river and ponder on the drama and sorrow and glory which had been the daily experience of Londoners in the last three years.

At the book stalls around St. Paul's Churchyard he looked in vain for his crony, the bookseller. A young man who kept the stall said the old fellow had died.

"Might you wish a recent pamphlet on matters of religion, sir?" he asked. "A fresh one comes in every day, like a hot bun."

Roger stared at the array of booklets. Many were in Latin. The name of one author struck a faint chord of memory. He picked up the volume signed by his name. Its title was *Reason of Church Government*.

"There, sir," said the salesman, "is a mighty fellow for writing. Mr. John Milton feeds King Pym arguments against the bishops.

He hath the boldest pen of all."

Roger did not answer. He was reading intently, caught by the sweep of the prose.

"This Mr. John Milton, sir," urged the bookseller, "writes in Latin too, and some say he hath writ poetry."

Repetition of the name suddenly brought a picture to Roger's mind. He was back in Cambridge, following a dissertation by a younger student. He could see a tall young man with white skin and fair hair delivering a brilliant speech in Latin. Paying for the book, Roger walked on wondering about the author.

He was to meet "the mighty fellow for writing." But not until after many days crammed with other matters. Even though Roger knew nothing could be done at the moment, he presented to Parliament his petition for a charter to be granted Providence and Rhode Island. In doing so he had a chance to talk to John Pym.

Pym looked worn and ill, but his eyes burned with the zeal of work. He remembered that Sir Edward Coke had been his visitor's friend and said, "When we abolished the Star Chamber and the High Commission, Sir Edward's life work was rewarded. From now on the Common Law shall rule."

It was the Earl of Warwick who received Roger's petition. The Earl, as proprietor of the Connecticut Valley tract, was deeply interested in all the new arrival could tell him of the federation of the four Colonies. He also wanted to hear about Roger's own experiment in free government.

Meanwhile, in his varied comings and goings Roger had renewed acquaintance with Edward Whalley, brother of the girl he had once adored. Without a pang of that youthful ardor he learned that Jane had married a minister, emigrated to New England, and lived in the colony of Plymouth. Whalley was eloquent about the mighty sweep of events in the nation.

"My faith, Mr. Williams," he cried, "the truth about this war is little understood. The force of it comes from religion."

As Roger made a surprised gesture of protest, Whalley said emphatically, "Aye, what lies below the people's clamor for a voice in government? Religion! Remember how the King forced down all that Puritans desired. In secret the doctrine spread and with it rebellion. Since this Parliament met, a miracle takes place. At first Archbishop Laud still ruled England. Now, with Parliament in power, Episcopalians have small voice against the general shout."

The shout came from throats of Presbyterians who wanted a national church. But another voice had recently been heard. Independents, the forerunners of Congregationalists, thought each church should be a free, voluntary organization.

"Mr. John Milton leans toward independency, as does Oliver Cromwell and his Ironsides," said Whalley. "But Mr. Milton argues for a general control of churches under a synod. As a Separatist, Mr. Williams, you might affect John Milton's views, did you talk to him."

At last one day in late August Roger Williams went to the small house in Aldersgate Street where lived the writer of pamphlets. The room in which they talked was piled with books and papers and lacked all order. Roger knew that Milton's recent bride had run away from him back to her family and that he lived by himself. Already there was suffering in the face of this lonely man who was to become one of the great poets of all time.

The bitterness of personal disappointments, the savage war of words he had been waging, had shadowed his deep-set eyes and drawn lines about his mouth.

But when the talk turned from politics and the church to literature, the whole man changed. A light from within made his very skin look glowing. He spoke of the poem he wished to write and, warmed by his visitor's sympathy, began to tell him about it.

"I think of some epic of man," said he with grave ardor, "of innocent man in his true body uncorrupted. Then would I paint his fall through Lucifer's contriving and all the grief in Heaven thereby. The drama would depict man's evil days and slow repentance of sin. Mercy, sweet servant of the Lord, brings comfort to his pain. Adam, knowing he must leave Paradise, first resents his fate, but learns through celestial beings to accept it lovingly. 'Tis then he can receive the Archangel's promise of a Messiah who would come to all men on earth."

The deep voice rolled out like a chant. It caused the walls of the small house to disappear. Across the open sky mighty pictures passed—the battle of angelic spirits, the flaming sword before the gate of Paradise, the thunderous music of Michael's prophecy. Roger observed the vision in awed silence.

After a time the poet said reflectively, "I have other themes. But I dream most of this one, of Paradise lost. It has been touched upon by writers in Holland. Would I could understand their language."

"Mayhap there I could help you, Mr. Milton. I speak and read a little Dutch."

His offer was instantly accepted and an hour was set for study together. Then Roger mentioned his need of a printer for his book on the Indian language and was told that Gregory Dexter was an excellent man.

A few days later a ship from Boston carried to Roger report of a terrible event. The Algonquin uprising in New Amsterdam had brought a tragic end to a notable life. With a shock of horror he read that Anne Hutchinson and her children had been massacred. As he learned that the attack was partly due to the fact that Governor Kieft had never turned over to the Indians the money she had paid for her farm, indignation made him cry aloud, "Perfidious rascal!"

Sorrowfully he reflected that this martyr's crown was set upon a life of ceaseless hardship. Yet it was a glorious life. Anne Hutchinson's fearless stand for truth as she saw it—this, together with her remarkable gifts, set her apart from all the women of her day.

That he must tell Sir Harry Vane of his friend's dreadful death clouded Roger's joy when he received a summons from the diplomat. He was back in London and sent at once for Roger.

With both hands outstretched, Vane cried in a warm tone, "Now by the Grace of God are we met again!"

Responding with heartfelt affection, Roger noted that the handsome youth who had taken New England by storm now wore an air of authority which gave him new stature. His mission had succeeded. The people of Scotland were alarmed by the intrigue of King Charles to persuade the Irish to help him attack the Scottish rebels. The latter realized that their only safety was to combine with the English Parliamentary forces.

"As you know," said Vane, flinging himself into a chair by the fire, "a covenant has been prepared by one of the Scottish leaders. It is a pledge to bring about unity in religion and civil liberties between their people and ours. Their Parliament has already signed the covenant and soon the House of Commons, at Pym's urging, will swear to it also. When that is done the doughty Scots will join us in the field of battle."

The two men exchanged a look of thanksgiving. It was a great moment shared. Even then they both half guessed that this union would prove the doom of the royalist party.

Sir Harry then pressed his friend for a report of the Colony. He wanted all the details of organizing the government. But when he learned of Anne Hutchinson's fate, it was some time before he could master his sorrow.

"It need not have been!" cried Roger with passionate conviction. "Dutch policy and English policy toward the savages lack all will to peace and understanding. Justice is not their guide. I am fearful, Sir Harry, of what trouble may befall the Narragansetts in my absence."

That fear was justified. When he saw Vane again, it was to bring him another tragic tale. This time it concerned Miantonomo. In the battle against the Mohegans for which he was setting out just as Roger left Providence, the Narragansett sachem had been captured. Uncas, with sly assurance, had asked the central council of the four Colonies what he should do with his foe. The officials gave him permission to put Miantonomo to death and promised the executioner protection against vengeance.

"It was betrayal of the wickedest kind!" Roger looked at young Vane with tears of sorrow and anger glistening in his dark eyes. "Miantonomo had stood by all the Colonies in their war against the Pequots. For this alone he deserved mercy—albeit he had broken his promise not to fight his enemy. Ah, sir, the English have stood behind all the evil Uncas hath done!"

Vane nodded. "'Tis a deadly game they play—and territory is the stake. You are the one true friend of the savages. But you work against odds."

For his part, Vane had cheering news to impart of the battle-field. A force was attacking the royal troops besieging Bristol, and Parliament dared hope for success. Shortly after this conversation Roger watched the good news burst over London.

He was in Westminster Abbey one afternoon when suddenly the great bell began to ring. Other bells took up the clamor. Shouts in the street were followed by roar of cannon from the Tower. Rushing into the square, he saw a crowd pelting to Westminster Hall. Already people were on the roof tops. Flags were waving. And now the cheers began. The name of the commander, Essex, shot into the air like a rocket to fall in glory of applause. Thus the city celebrated the raising of the siege of Bristol.

On those good tidings London had to nourish hope for months. Further action awaited the training of more Parliamentary troops. It was a waiting period, also, for the ambassador from Providence. Hearings on his petition dawdled. He found it hard to be patient when he knew that Hugh Peters was trying to influence the Council against him. And Peters had powerful help from America.

It was by no mere chance that just then on all the book stalls appeared a pamphlet written by John Cotton. It explained why Roger Williams had been banished from the commonwealth and offered pious defense of severe measures against heretics and agitators. The very first day Roger saw it he heard Cotton's argument quoted admiringly by one of the stern Presbyterian divines.

Immediately Roger began to write an answer to Cotton. But thanks to interruptions, 1644 began before he had finished his paper. With the new year came a packet of letters from America with an account of dire happenings at Shawomet. Massachusetts was in action there also! In a frenzy of despair, he rushed to Sir Harry Vane and poured out his fury.

In November Boston magistrates had sent to Shawomet an armed force to bring Samuel Gorton and his followers before the General Court. When they refused to go, they were put in chains and taken as prisoners to Boston. The crops of the settlement were carried off or burned. The women and children fled into the forest or piled into boats. Most of them received shelter in Portsmouth or Providence. But fright and exposure caused the death of John Greene's wife and another woman. Several of the refugees had been brought to death's door by their cruel experiences.

Young Vane listened in horror to this account. "The Holy Commonwealth!" he exclaimed at last. " 'Tis more arbitrary than King Charles himself. This wickedness shall be reported to the Commission on the Colonies!"

That body had been appointed the previous November. And according to Edward Whalley, who hurried over to Roger's rooms to tell him about it, the men on the Commission were the very ones to help him.

"Your friends are in control, Mr. Williams," Whalley had reported triumphantly. "The Earl of Warwick heads the Commission. Sir Harry Vane and Oliver Cromwell and others who wish you well are on it. Be at ease as to your petition's being swiftly taken up."

By that time Roger's little book about the Indians, *Key into the Language of America,* had made a distinct impression. Members of Parliament and of the Assembly and even business men who had put money into American ventures were reading it.

Among the many congratulations given the author none was warmer than Lady Vane's. "Your book," said she, "did—I confess to my shame—give me my first knowledge that Indians are truly God's creations and not mere fearful enemies of Englishmen. 'Tis a composition full of wisdom and delight."

Blushing with pleasure, he said, "Ah, madam, I drew the materials in a rude lump at sea, that I might not lose what I had so dearly bought among the barbarians."

Laughing at his modesty, Sir Harry's wife went on. "What I liked best was your story of the Indian who heard your preaching and who said as he was dying, 'Your words were never out of my heart.' I shall tell Oliver Cromwell of your 'spiritual observations.'"

Many people must have spoken to that man of destiny about Roger Williams. For Cromwell greeted the agent of the Narragansett country with a cordiality which their former acquaintance could not quite explain. The two men met in November at Sir Harry Vane's house when the Colonel had come up to London to confer with Pym.

None of the other leaders seemed to Roger so indomitable as Cromwell. Not because of his appearance nor his manner. Often silent and always grave, he made no show of power. Nor had he need to do so. It was there, secret and irresistible, like the force of wind or the sea.

With abrupt sincerity Cromwell began to question Roger, first as to the meaning of the term Seeker and then about the kind of government set up in Providence. His eyes widened with interest to hear Roger's clear argument for complete liberty of conscience.

The next time Roger saw Cromwell, the strange, heavy face was streaming with tears. But most eyes were wet at that funeral ceremony for the great John Pym. He was dead—King Pym, whose plans for government, for religious reform, for union with the Scots, and for military strategy had guided liberal England for three crucial years! Many men declared that all plans would fail without him. But the real leaders knew better than that. Pym's work had been done so well, his campaign so clearly mapped out, that now others could carry on. And it was plain even in the early months of 1644 that the individual most likely to assume control of events was Oliver Cromwell.

Loss of Pym marked the opening of a sad and bitter winter for London. Never was such cold. King Charles had possession of the town of Newcastle where lay the coal mines, and none of it could be had in the capital. Men with country properties had sleigh-loads of wood brought in to their houses and to rented chambers. But poor people had to suffer and freeze.

One icy day Roger was returning from John Milton's house. Milton had just published his treatise defending divorce, and it had shocked every conservative in the Assembly and in the House of Commons. He was, therefore, more alone than ever and Roger spent what time with him he could spare. On the way home he got his first impression of the average Londoner's piteous state.

Around a small, neglected church he saw a ragged crowd. Through the open door came the sound of ax blades splintering through wood. Curiosity made him stop and edge his way through the press.

"What goes on within?" he asked an unshaven young fellow.

Through lips blue with cold the youth answered in an excited voice. "Lads with axes do chop up the church pews for us to burn. There'll be enough wood to keep us alive for a bit."

All the pioneer blood in Roger rose up in protest. Church pews! There were forests not so many miles from London. Was there no means of using such supply to relieve this distress? Before he reached his rooms he had thought out a plan. With the help of some business men he had met on the Board of Trade he proceeded next day to work it out.

Thus it was that one afternoon near sunset several men just leaving Parliament beheld a strange procession. A train of carts piled high with untrimmed trees and fallen logs made its creaking way through the streets. Seated beside the driver of the first team was a figure in tall black hat and woolen cloak strangely familiar to the group.

"Look, sirs!" cried one of the observers. "Do I mistake, or is that Mr. Williams of Providence Plantations riding on the cart?"

Edward Whalley, who was in the party, uttered a surprised laugh. " 'Tis he, indeed. He appears to bring a wood supply to London. Perhaps he went back to Providence to fetch it! Hah, there's a man of action!"

Later Roger told Whalley that he had spent no better hours in England than in directing the gathering of that dead wood for the poor of London.

It was, however, not as a man of action but as a radical thinker that he captured attention. In February he published through

Gregory Dexter two pamphlets fated to be widely read on both sides of the ocean. *Mr. Cotton's Letter Examined and Answered* was the first. With no personal bitterness about his own fate, the author showed how unchristian were the persecutions in New England. A second pamphlet, addressed to Parliament, the Church of Scotland, and the dissenters in the Westminster Assembly, was an attack against a national church.

Gregory Dexter had come to agree with his patron's arguments and was very proud of the excitement they aroused.

"You tread upon Presbyterian toes, sir!" said he. "But there will be gnashing of teeth when the third book comes from the press. From the chapters I have seen, it hath the most force."

This booklet was not yet completed. Even when it was, Roger thought best to delay publication until the eve of his return to America. He didn't wish to put a pebble in the way of getting the charter. Wasn't Massachusetts strewing rocks across that path? Sir Harry Vane told Roger that he suspected some scheme of the Bay Company was being hatched and that he was watching carefully. Roger was staying at Vane's house at the time and the two men spent much time discussing how problems of government had best be solved.

Into the study where Roger was working on his pamphlet Sir Harry strode one late afternoon. "Look you, friend!" he cried in great excitement. "Mr. Hugh Peters and his assistant have almost succeeded in a fraud. They drew up a paper increasing the grant of Massachusetts to extend over the entire tract of Narragansett Bay. By some means nine members of the Commission signed the false document."

"Signed it?" echoed Roger, dumbfounded. "Did nine men connive with theft?"

Vane was stripping off his gauntlet gloves and tossing them into his hat. He had something of the gay, graceful swagger belonging rather to the Cavalier than to the Roundhead.

"Nay," he replied, "the nine signers thought the paper an honest one. It was cleverly tricked out with seals. But do not be troubled. The fraud will never even come up for passage."

This was no empty boast. The forged grant was suppressed. Moreover, Roger's own patent was soon passed. It allowed everything for which the petitioners had asked. The officials called the grant, "a free Charter of civil incorporation and government to the Providence Plantations on Narragansett Bay." The possession of private land bought from Indians was authorized and Roger's main political principles were approved—government, springing from the people, devoted to protecting human rights and defending the general welfare.

At a private session Roger was congratulated by the Duke of Warwick, Vane, and Cromwell. The latter said, "To my knowledge this is the first free charter of government given to a Colony of England. Other Colonies have trading patents or they belong to great proprietors. May your experiment prosper, Mr. Williams!"

Even when deeply stirred Roger was always a realist. "Truly, sirs," said he, "a government based on consent by those governed hath no smooth way before it. Yet I believe such is the only true compact."

Better than anyone else Cromwell knew what a powerful influence this American had become. When the Colonel of the Ironsides talked with his men around the campfire, he heard them quoting Roger Williams. All free-thinking groups—Levelers, Seekers, Diggers—considered him their champion. Radicals read his pamphlets, sought private interviews with him, and spread his doctrine of personal liberty.

Only a few intimates knew the price paid for principle. All spring a lawsuit to recover the Williams inheritance was dragging on in the courts. At last there seemed a chance to win and the brothers took heart. But in the end Roger lost his share.

"I could not swear the oath asked by the Court," he explained to Sir Harry. " 'Twas the same thing I opposed in Boston. To swear a civil oath in the name of God doth confuse civil and spiritual matters. On that I could not waver."

Young Vane gave him a look of reverent admiration. How many men would sacrifice an inheritance to uphold such a principle? Especially after paying out large sums to win the charter for his Colony!

Roger's pamphlet was now on the stalls and hundreds of Londoners were talking of little else. *The Bloody Tenet* they called it for short. The real title, half a page in length, began with the words, "The Bloody Tenet of Persecution for Cause of Conscience discussed in a Conference Between Truth and Peace." With picturesque eloquence the author preached that bloodshed and torture perpetrated in the name of religion were the exact contrary of Christ's teaching.

When the time came to part, Sir Harry Vane said, "You will doubtless hear, my friend, perhaps even before your ship sails, how wickedly this latest product of your pen has been received by some in Parliament. We are hard pushed there by Presbyterians, both Scotch and English, to show less tolerance for other forms of religion. These men cry out against the independency of *The Bloody Tenet*. For reasons of politics Parliament will vote, I fear, to burn a copy of your book."

"Burn it!" Roger looked shocked to the heart.

" 'Tis a bad reward for all you have taught men in this town of sound government and brotherhood. But the ugly deed is of little moment. You have stirred up a love of liberty that will never burn away!"

If such were the case, thought Roger, no man would ask a better reward for his work. Indeed, when he boarded the schooner, it was with a feeling of being a rich man. His mission had succeeded and he had gleaned a wealth of experience and friendship.

One of his converts stood beside him on the deck, bound for America. Gregory Dexter had sold his business and joined his fortunes with this advocate of a better order of society. Another, equally convinced, planned to follow later. He had the same name as the Providence miller, John Smith. Many men in London had come to bid Williams regretful farewell and to tell him how much encouragement and instruction he had given them. It had been glorious to share for a while the mighty struggle in his native land. But now he was impatient to return to America where lay his own life work.

Gregory Dexter turned from watching the last of England's coast. "Mr. Williams, what will most gladden you in reaching the New World again?"

Roger's face lighted with eagerness. "To see my baby son, born last December, whom I have never held in my arms."

13

HOMECOMING from afar is ever a deep experience. For Roger Williams, arrival on the American coast was filled with drama. In the first place, he had a letter from the Parliamentary Commission requesting his safe passage through Massachusetts. Therefore he took a ship which anchored in Boston harbor.

Permission to come ashore was accompanied by a request that Mr. Williams call upon Governor Winthrop. Graciously received in the executive's big, cool room, Roger noted with a keen glance how the pioneer hut had changed in the last decade. The house now had every air of comfort and even touches of elegance. Less happy was the impression given by the Governor himself. His face had grown at once sadder and more severe. Evidently practice of power had filched something from his lovable humanity.

Roger asked affectionately for the health of both the Winthrops. He always took for granted their strong mutual friendship in spite of disagreement about religion, politics, and the Indians.

Yet, even as he spoke, two accusing figures seemed to rise up between him and the Governor. One, the slain sachem of the Narragansetts; the other, Samuel Gorton.

"Aye, Mr. Williams," said the executive in answer to his visitor's question. "Despite his errors and his stubborn violence, Mr. Gorton has felt our clemency. He has been released and doubtless you will find him at Providence among others who tilt at windmills."

The Governor's tone was mildly sarcastic. It justified all that the authorities of Massachusetts had done at Shawomet. Breaking up homes and imprisoning the leaders of a group living outside the Colony was apparently quite in keeping with this man's conscience. Gorton had defied the General Court. To do so was to defy an ordinance of God. For it was the duty of God's chosen representatives to suppress such noisy, free-thinking upstarts as Gorton and his followers.

As he traced the unspoken argument, Roger was filled with sudden pity for John Winthrop. This good and influential man was giving his life to oppose the tide of democracy and freedom of thought rising in the world. Cromwell was preaching to his soldiers around the campfire the worth and dignity of each man's independent soul. To his last gasp Pym had worked for those principles of political liberty underlying the Reformation. Yet Winthrop could feel no breath of new ideas upon his cheek. He still believed with John Cotton that aristocrats should rule the people as viceregents of Heaven.

"Gorton now mixes in the Narragansett affair," went on the Governor in a wrathful tone. "He hath helped persuade Canonicus, the chief, to swear fealty to Parliament direct. Now the sachem refuses to treat with our Colony and threatens fresh war on the Mohegans. This means danger to all."

Fire flashed in Roger's eyes. "Your misguidings are great and lamentable," he said. "You of this Colony share the bad judgment of Connecticut concerning the worth of the fox, Uncas. Do you strive like a Christian to show the Indians a better justice than they mete out to one another? Nay. You would agree with the Dutch of New Amsterdam who said to me, 'Better that a thousand of these heathen dogs be killed than Christians be endangered or troubled.'"

Over Winthrop's dignified face passed a half smile. It dealt tolerantly with this fanatic. Gravely he suggested that Roger go to see his savage friend and try to soothe his wrath. He then gave the conversation a personal turn by asking for mutual friends in London.

Naturally the Governor knew that Parliament had granted a charter for the new Colony. Before he left London, Roger had learned that Massachusetts was recalling its agents there because they had not prevented this action. As the two men bade one another good-by, they exchanged an affectionate smile across a widening gulf of opposition.

Before he left Boston, Roger visited a number of old friends. They were eager to hear about the civil war in England and of the work of the Westminster Assembly. Yet, much as he enjoyed these sociable hours, he was eager to be on his way.

At Seekonk a surprise welcome awaited him. Fourteen canoes full of people from Providence and Portsmouth had come up there to escort him back in triumph. Gregory Dexter was delighted over such a demonstration offered in the midst of the wilderness. With cheers and congratulations they put Roger in the central canoe and swept him down to be greeted by the rest of his fellow townsmen.

For the traveler, however, the climax of the journey came when the door of his own house at last closed behind him. Mary in his arms crying, "Roger, Roger, my dear husband!" Little figures clustering around him, small hands pulling at the skirts of his tunic. Shrill voices shouting, "Father!" And through the happy din one sound which he had longed to hear—a gurgling crow from Joseph, the baby he now saw for the first time.

Late that evening Roger and Mary were still talking over the last fourteen months. Things had gone well for both farm and family. Everyone had been kind.

"And now," concluded Mary happily, "with a charter to unite the towns, there will be peace in the Colony."

Roger shook his head with a twisted smile. "Nay, my dear wife, have no such dream. 'Tis my prediction that Rhode Island men will not like the charter. Nor will the other Colonies cease to push their claims against us. We shall have discord yet for many years."

To be so forewarned was a help. For Roger's prophecy came true to the letter. Few were satisfied with the charter. Although it raised Rhode Island and Providence Plantations to equal status with the other four Colonies, it made the residents dependent on Parliament. No longer could the towns enter into separate alliances or declare war against an Indian tribe or grant franchises. Such limitations galled the Arnolds and the Harris group and ambitious leaders of Newport. Some of these uneasy citizens appealed to Massachusetts to oppose the government of Providence. Assemblies were stormy. Angry letters passed back and forth. Roger spent hours trying to soothe the discontents.

No wonder there was a glow on his worn, patient face when he said to Mary, "Today I go to the camp of old Canonicus. My red-skinned brothers may have many complaints. But theirs are usually just and reasonable."

It was good to be alone again in the pinnace, sailing over the silent waters. Wind in the pines and hemlocks, wind visible in the whorls of cloud scudding over the mighty sky—how it suggested the voice of the Guardian of Earth. To listen, to observe the miracles of plant and rock, was the way to learn of the Creator. It was better than sermonizing by the most eloquent preacher.

After dropping anchor, he took the trail. The Narragansett village always moved itself up in the hills for the summer and it was a long, long walk to camp. The moment he approached the clearing, one of the watchers ran ahead, and by the time Roger reached the great pine tree where the sachem held his council, the chiefs were gathered there in state. A tense air of challenge held them all in silence as Roger stretched out his arm in greeting and spoke the customary words, "What cheer, *Nétop?*"

Canonicus arose and looked long into the face of his friend. Those soft, sad eyes told the Narragansett that Roger had suffered over the execution of Miantonomo. For an instant the two men felt they were together in sorrow against all who had caused the young man's death. Then the Englishman began to speak.

"Even this deed must be forgiven, great chief," Roger slowly felt out the Indian words he had not used for so long. "Men slew the Son of God on a cross, yet have they received infinite mercy. Let us not make war. Let us talk around the peace table like sons of the starry heaven."

Moved in spite of his longing for vengeance, the Indian turned to his younger nephew. Pessicus now stood in the place of Miantonomo. He had not the noble beauty of his dead brother. As he stood with folded arms looking down at his visitor, all the cruelty of which his race was capable cast his face in stone. Suddenly the blade of his words struck fire from that stone.

Passionately he declared that Uncas must pay for his crime against the Narragansetts. With graphic gestures he outlined the lies and treachery of his enemy. Nor did he spare the white men of Connecticut and Massachusetts who had supported the evil chief of the Mohegans and had permitted the death of the noble sachem. Pessicus had sent word to the Court of Massachusetts that unless Uncas stood trial for the murder of Miantonomo, war would be declared on the Mohegans.

Listening with deep sympathy to this savage outburst, Roger repeated silently to himself, " 'Ye have heard that it hath been said, Thou shalt love thy neighbor, and hate thine enemy. But I say unto you, Love your enemies . . . and pray for them that persecute you.' "

To hear the grunts of approval accorded Pessicus, to see the light of battle in the eye of every chief in the council, convinced Roger that talk of peace was idle. With a sigh he arose. At least he could plead for postponement of the war. Let it not come until after the next planting time. Let the fruitful earth have its way for all the innocent before blood be shed.

His eloquence won him a respectful hearing. At last he drew from the council a reluctant consent to delay the attack. What persuaded the Narragansetts, as they frankly said, was the man himself. For a dear and trusted friend of the tribe they would do as he asked.

Still another tribute was paid the ambassador from Providence. He discussed with Canonicus and his nephew a new plan he had for trading. Greatly in need of funds and of rebuilding his trade, he wanted to set up a post right in the heart of the Narragansett country on the western shore of Narragansett Bay.

As they listened to this proposal, the faces of the two Indian sachems filled with joy. "Good to have friend near us," they said. "Welcome to our country, friend."

Before he left, Roger gathered all who cared to listen and preached to them of the goodness and mercy of God. He prayed with them and asked them to pray.

At the end of the session, one of the younger princes said to him shyly, "You not ask us give up our gods. You not ask us be Christians. We hear of your gods. We worship together. That is good."

Repeating this comment to his friends, the ministers, at Providence, Roger said, "In Boston I heard much of the work of Mr. John Eliot. He has converted a group of Indians to Christianity. That I cannot do. I cannot use my own will upon their beliefs. Mr. Eliot is translating the Bible into the Indian tongue and mayhap that will help us all. But I have little faith in conversion of these heathen—unless it be slow and through example."

During the spring of 1645 Roger started his trading post. Where the town of Wickford now stands, some twenty miles below Providence, he built his log hut and a wharf. Gradually he cleared ground around the building. With rose bushes along the path, hollyhocks about the hut, a little vegetable garden where pease and beans and sweet corn grew, the little outpost slowly came to have the look of a small country estate. Before many seasons passed, Mary and the children came to pay him long visits there. The youngsters played with the children of the Narragansett tribe and learned from them woodcraft, basket weaving.

and other useful things. When Mrs. Williams had to look after the house in Providence, young Mary stayed with her father.

Gregory Dexter, whose own house in the town was soon finished, helped his friend build the trading post. Although the printer rapidly became an active citizen and skillful farmer, he found one phase of pioneer living a great trial. That was the nearness of the explosive Indian tribes. He was often uneasy about the risks his friend ran. The bloody war which Pessicus conducted against the Mohegans went on far from the settlements. It ended in the complete defeat of Uncas and for months no further disturbance occurred. But when it came to settling the peace terms, Roger was drawn in immediately.

One summer day in 1646, Roger and Gregory Dexter were happily engaged in a special task. They were helping with advice and letters of introduction to get Samuel Gorton off to London. Gorton had decided to ask Parliament in person to protect his lands and liberty from Massachusetts. Roger had equipped him with notes to the Duke of Warwick, Sir Harry Vane, and other influential men. Dexter was advising him about lodgings.

In the midst of the conference a runner from Pessicus appeared. Watching his friend as he conversed in the Narragansett tongue with the messenger, Dexter grew anxious.

"What is wanted, Mr. Williams?" he asked as the Indian sat down to partake of refreshment. "Why do you look so grave?"

It was a strange request Pessicus had made. For months he had refused to accept Roger's advice to talk over peace terms with the officials of Massachusetts. They had demanded that the Narragansett sachem personally answer to them for making war against a tribe friendly to the United Colonies. Roger had said the conference was essential to a settled peace. Now at last Pessicus had made up his mind to go. But on one condition. This was that Roger serve as hostage for his life and safety.

"Hostage?" repeated Dexter with a horrified look at Roger. "You mean, you must stay helpless at the heathen camp and yield up your life if harm come to Pessicus?"

"Aye," replied Roger coolly, "but I doubt if I must pay any forfeit. My serving as hostage will assure the sachem's safety. Mr. Winthrop would do nought to cause my death."

No argument could keep the friend of the Narragansetts from undertaking this mission. Laying aside personal affairs and civic duties, he spent a fortnight with the tribe, living their life, preaching to them, and inspecting furs for his trading business.

One afternoon a white man with two Indian guides from the tribe of Massasoit came into camp. He was a servant indentured to one of the members of the Massachusetts General Court. Brought to the tent of Canonicus where Roger was talking with a group of youths, the stranger drew from his pouch a letter addressed to Mr. Roger Williams of Providence Plantations.

Canonicus stared at the missive with passionate anxiety. Was it bad news about Pessicus—that was the question in his eyes.

Swiftly Roger broke the seal. As he read, color rose in his cheeks. Signed by all members of the General Court, the letter informed Roger that nearly three years before, on December 10, 1643, the High Court of Parliament had granted to the Massachusetts Bay Company all the lands about Narragansett Bay including Providence and Aquidneck or Rhode Island.

Ah, yes! This was the thieving scheme which Sir Harry Vane had nipped in the bud. Roger knew all about it. Hadn't he been in London at the time? What a stupid deceit on the part of the educated gentlemen of the Court! How dared they try such a trick?

All at once Roger became aware of the sachem's fixed gaze. Hurriedly he assured him that no news of Pessicus was in the letter. It concerned the receiver alone.

"My friend has face of thunder," commented Canonicus. "Bad news for him?"

Before he could reply, the servant remarked stolidly, "Tomorrow, Mr. Williams, I must go back with your answer."

"Take your ease then, good man," said Roger politely. "I shall prepare my answer at once."

Not only to the General Court did Roger write, but to John Winthrop and to his son and to the president of the Providence government. Addressing each one lovingly, he denounced the supposed grant as a bare-faced forgery and assured all and sundry that the petition of Massachusetts to control Narragansett Bay territory had never passed the Commission, let alone Parliament. With such firmness and authority did he expose the forgery of the supposed grant that it was finally dropped.

A few days after this amazing incident Pessicus returned. To the ceremonies of his reception he made little response. With the air of one stricken to the heart he reported the conditions handed out by the Massachusetts magistrates. That a chief victorious in battle had had to accept such terms marked the depth of humiliation demanded by English power.

First, Pessicus had to pay 2,000 fathoms of Indian money to the Federation and leave three royal hostages indefinitely in Massachusetts. Second, he had to promise that he would not again break the peace with Uncas.

Glancing at the bowed head of Canonicus, Roger shared the sachem's bitterness. Proudly had the chief ruled a superior people until the English came to America. Even then he was ready to be friendly to the strangers and had proved it in the first Pequot War. But what was the good of friendly feeling if the treacherous enemy, Uncas, was always favored at his expense? Only trouble, thought Roger mournfully, much trouble, would follow such an unjust settlement.

In spite of discouragements from many quarters, Roger found the next years richly rewarding. His children were growing helpful and companionable. His farm prospered and the swine and goats he was breeding, together with his trade, gave him an adequate living. Meanwhile London friends kept him in close touch with events of the civil war.

One of the turning points was reached shortly after he had sailed for America in 1644. In July Cromwell, marching north near York, had defeated the King's forces in the terrific battle of Marston Moor. Roger, whose pamphlet *The Bloody Tenet* had been burned by Parliament, saw a definite connection between this victory in the field and the publication of Milton's pamphlet defending freedom of the press. Called by the Greek title, *Areopagitica*, after the famous hill near Athens where St. Paul preached, the paper fought a mighty battle of its own against the forces which would snuff out the expression of thought.

Cromwell, now head of a magnificently trained army, won another battle in June 1645. This victory at Naseby utterly routed the Cavaliers. With 5,000 prisoners taken, the Royalist cause looked hopeless. Yet his very success brought the victor new enemies. Parliamentarians and Presbyterians had begun to fear his power. His Ironsides were devoted to the cause of independence in religion and democracy in government. Would they control all England?

Roger Williams thought deeply about these tremendous events. Many an evening did he spend discussing them with his friends.

"Defeat of the King is certain," he would say, "but it will not bring peace to England. No more there than here in Narragansett Bay can men learn to use freedom in a day."

Bitter quarrels were dividing the Colony. Appointed mediator of land disputes, Roger worked with loving patience to obtain justice and hold greed at bay. He insisted that common lands be held open for new settlers and that poor men with small allotments keep a quarter right to the pastures. With equal firmness he defended encroachments against the Colony. Backed by the Union, Massasoit suddenly put in a claim for lands near Providence, but withdrew it when Roger faced him down with his own deceit.

So it went until 1647. Long before then Samuel Gorton and his friends had come back from England with everything they wanted from the Duke of Warwick's Commission. Massachusetts was handed written orders to cease interfering with the settlers of Shawomet, and they promptly moved back to their lands, rebuilt their houses, restocked their farms and began life again. In honor of the helpful Duke the town was named Warwick. Such success was gall and wormwood to the groups headed by the Arnolds and by William Harris. Under the protection of Massachusetts, these enemies of Gorton annoyed him all they could and so did the Indians of the district. Several times Roger had to hurry over to Warwick to prevent active warfare.

These continual disturbances and the haughty refusal of William Coddington of Newport to co-operate in upholding the charter had a counterpart outside Narragansett Bay. Signs of Dutch hostility were more frequent. Rumor had it that Connecticut and Rhode Island might be invaded. A feeling of helpless anxiety began to seep through the Colony. Everywhere people began asking, "How can we take any measures of defense when the towns will not unite?"

At last a number of leaders suggested that a mutual conference of all residents be called. In May 1647 a general assembly attended by most of the men of the Colony was held at Portsmouth. It was the beginning of a genuine attempt to set up a workable government. Other assemblies followed which were really constitutional conventions. Those who took part in them laid the corner stone of America's future.

With what inner excitement Roger Williams worked out the program of that first historic meeting. He was not only Moderator for the whole assembly, but was chairman of a committee of ten representing the town of Providence with full power to act.

Those who paddled over with him across the Bay that morning never forgot the impression he made. It was a beautiful dawn and the light of it was in Roger's face. From time to time he looked about proudly at the small fleet of boats making its way to Portsmouth. On shore a committee of citizens met the newcomers and the place was buzzing with sociability. A large number of Newport residents had already arrived and soon the men from Warwick and the turbulent inhabitants of Pawtuxet lands were on the scene.

The gathering had something of the air of a big Sunday School picnic or Grange meeting of modern times. People ate out of doors and every instant greeted old acquaintances or made new ones. Between each session everyone relaxed and made merry.

The primary task of the Assembly was to reaffirm faith in the charter. Everyone—even William Coddington—signed full agreement with its terms. Warwick was formally admitted to membership with all the rights possessed by other towns. A tentative body of laws was worked out and committees were appointed to draw up a civil code. Most important of all was discussion of the complete governmental system now emerging clear for the first time.

"According to this design," explained Roger Williams, "there will be a general government ministering to the Colony as a whole. But each town has its own separate government to watch sharply for the rights and interests of citizens. No town officer should also serve the central body."

It was to Williams that everyone looked for guidance. They knew that years of thought and study had gone into his shaping of the plan. Even his opponents, who feared the strength of his will, had to admit that his purpose was without self-interest. What was achieved for the Colony in those early days was a kind of overture for the Constitution of the United States.

The executive branch consisted of a President and four Assistants, one from each town. The General Court enforced the adopted code of laws. But each town could agitate for or against a certain law and if a majority of the whole Colony disapproved of a measure, it could be repealed.

A preamble to this early constitution set forth the principle of liberty of conscience. It outlined the human rights which were to be defended by the federal government. As the people's instrument, the state was empowered to punish offenders against the peace, defend the Colony by arbitration or by force against aggression, and undertake a variety of positive work for the common interests of all citizens.

As the first session of this great enterprise drew to a close, Roger Williams arose to address the convention.

"The two inestimable jewels of a people are peace and liberty of persons. No life or limb shall be taken from us except by known laws and agreements of our own making."

He paused for a breath of thankfulness that these citizens need never dread the secret tyranny of a Star Chamber. In the great spaces of the new land no dreadful Tower would loom up to imprison victims of an arbitrary rule.

"We of this Colony," he went on, "shall have liberty of estates, houses, lands, cattle, and goods. Not a penny shall be taken except after free debate among all and action taken by deputies sent by ourselves to the General Assembly. The civil and general magistrates are but the eyes, hands, and instruments of the people."

A triumphant sweetness stamped the face of the speaker. His far-gazing eyes held youthful fire. His body was erect and lightly poised. Yet he had the air of a person who had spared himself nothing. He had given his youth, his strength, all the power of his mind and heart, that this experiment in self-government might come to pass.

In the months that followed the May convention, Roger devoted every possible moment to work on various committees. "'Tis a fortunate matter," he said to Thomas James, "that so many good heads are at work amongst us. We have lawyers as shrewd as any in London and university men a-plenty."

"Aye, sir," agreed James, "and 'tis my opinion our code of laws will set a new pattern of justice. Yet, Mr. Williams, I have already heard murmurs against the power of the central government. The townsmen are afraid of it. They know not why, but it seems to put a shadow on their liberties."

William Coddington was one of those distrustful critics. As a means of educating him and at the same time using his energy for the common good, the Assembly elected Coddington president of the Colony at the May meeting of 1648.

In vain. A few months later the agitating news of this man's behavior ran through the Colony like wild fire. John Clark of Newport rushed up to Providence to report the facts to Roger Williams. Coddington had sent a petition to the United Colonies asking the Union to include him and promising to aid Massachusetts in trying to annex Warwick and all of Rhode Island.

"He cannot accept our democratic government," roared John Clark. "He wants to be king of Aquidneck. Can this treachery be tolerated, Mr. Williams, on the part of the Colony's president?"

"Nay, indeed!" responded Roger promptly. "A democracy must fight its enemies within."

That was the general opinion. Coddington was promptly suspended from office. Soon after this discipline the reply of Massachusetts was reported. The United Colonies refused to accept Coddington unless his whole would-be kingdom of Rhode Island submitted to the jurisdiction of Plymouth. Hoping that Newport's aristocrat would now see the light and learn to co-operate with the common folk, citizens of the island implored him to put his case before an impartial group of judges. Time after time Roger sailed over to the island in an attempt to arbitrate the difficulties. But Coddington remained aloof and superior. Refusing to arbitrate anything, he suddenly departed for England.

"He is up to no good," remarked Thomas Olney with skeptical calm.

"To whom will he appeal?" wondered Roger. "England is on the eve of a second civil war, from all I hear."

Charles First was now a prisoner on the Isle of Wight. The triumphant army of Cromwell, however, refused to disband. For the Ironsides intended to have something to say about the government they had fought to defend. It had narrowed down, that government, to a group of die-hard Presbyterians who did not represent England. The army demanded that it resign and that a new election be held. Parliament, fearing the Independents, stubbornly refused to do so and, indeed, sought a reconciliation with the King.

In the spring of 1649 tremendous news came to Providence from two quite different directions. First, a visitor from John Winthrop, Junior, reported a letter from Winthrop's father-in-law in England. Hugh Peters had become Cromwell's chaplain and had been present when Cromwell forcibly winnowed out what he considered the chaff of Parliament.

As members entered St. Stephen's Chapel one morning, they found the General's armed force at the door. An officer named Pride challenged each individual member and checked his name on a list. Everyone not approved by Cromwell was promptly arrested. This act was known as "Pride's Purge," and the fragment

of Parliament left to govern England was contemptuously dubbed
the Rump. From that time forward Oliver Cromwell was suspected of wishing to rule by arbitrary methods.

Roger Williams, the only man in Providence who knew Cromwell, was besieged with questions about this episode. But he refused to make a comment. He thought it one of the turns into
darkness which might alter the character of the glorious struggle
for freedom. The will to free their country from narrow and backward ideas had led the Ironsides to use the same arbitrary power
they had hated in the King.

The second piece of news was personally delivered to Roger.
He was down at his trading station on the coast. When a Dutch
ship hove to in the little harbor, he had rowed out with his packet
of furs for export. The moment he climbed on board he found
the captain bursting with excitement.

"What your country hath done now," shouted the Dutchman,
"ought to make Englishmen blush for horrid shame. They have
beheaded King Charles at Whitehall and all Europe shudders at
the outrage!"

Shocked to his marrow, Roger carried with him through all
the duties of the day the grim pictures described by the Dutch-
men of that execution. His daughter Mary, who was keeping
house for him at the trading post, found him strangely abstracted.
After supper he wrote the news to John Winthrop. Long had
Roger been convinced that Charles First had learned nothing
from the civil war. To the very last he clung to his Divine Right
to absolute power and made no terms with Parliament. Of the
King's execution, Roger wrote, " 'Tis true it is a dangerous rem-

edy, yet that which God used against Baal's priests."

Laying aside his quill, he said to Mary, "This may be my last letter to Mr. Winthrop. He is ill and not long for this world."

Mary glanced tenderly at her father. She thought his face with its deep lines and creases was a noble record of undaunted action.

"Father, thy days are so full. At dawn thou didst hoe the garden. Then came Narragansetts to see thee. When the Dutch ship came, thou wert a trader. Later matters of the central government kept thee hard at work. Tonight thou dost compose a letter. Of all these tasks, which is best to thy liking?"

Roger looked pleased at her interest. "All other duties seem but means to the one—that of government. Principles by which men may live sociably together are like pillars to a temple. Today, Mary, I worked on the code of punishments for misdeeds. These laws are merciful."

As he leaned forward, the candlelight showed the triumph in his face. "Daughter, dost thou know that our Colony is alone in this—we have no punishment for heresy, nor for breaking the Sabbath by working or playing games. Nor have we set any tithes for support of a church. Our Civil Code treats only of civil things."

Now, however, he could see that Mary was not listening. Her eyes were watching through the open door a shining patch of moonlight on the restless waters of the bay. She smiled as if at some romantic vision, and her father, watching her, smiled too. Then he turned back to his papers and drew out the manuscript of the Civil Code. Slowly he read again the finale which he had just composed:

*"These are the laws that concern all men,
and these are the penalties for the transgression
thereof, which by the common consent are
ratified and established throughout this whole
Colony; and otherwise than thus what is for-
bidden, all men may walk as their conscience
persuade them, every man in the name of his
god."*

A mighty power lay in the gentle words of this epilogue. They
were to influence other Colonies from that time forward. For
they put in plain terms two great principles—that of liberty of
conscience and that of democracy.

It was encouraging to Roger that every year more residents of
the Narragansett Bay section put heart into making the system of
government succeed. They were proud of it and jealous of threat
to its peaceful accomplishment. But such threat was never absent.
For in each of the four towns lived egoists who saw government
as an enemy to personal power.

Most vicious of all was William Harris. He had twisted the
terms of Miantonomo's original grant and forged documents to
prove his claim to huge tracts of land. Then he registered these
false deeds with the Massachusetts Court. His influence was destructive not only upon the whole matter of Colony expansion,
but upon other men. Benedict and William Arnold, Thomas Olney, and even John Smith, the man who had followed Roger
from England, were inspired by Harris to join his schemes and
to flout both Indian treaties and the Providence government.

Another enemy to the democratic system was William Coddington. In 1651 he had come back from England in triumph. Somehow he had wrested from the Council of State a full grant of power and a life governorship over the entire territory of Rhode Island. Thus the power of the 1644 Charter was cut almost in half. Naturally the majority of citizens on the island deeply resented having such autocratic rule imposed upon them.

From outside the Colony dangers also pressed. Time after time Williams had to use speed and skill to prevent Indian warfare from breaking out. Once Uncas actually had someone stab him in order to blame the deed on a young Narragansett. With this excuse he won from the New England Union a promise to send an armed force against his enemies. But Roger insisted on a formal hearing. Testimony proved that no Narragansett had wounded the Mohegan chief and war was avoided.

Another time the Union was enraged because Pessicus had fallen behind in the harsh payments imposed by the Boston treaty. A meeting was called to revise the terms and Williams was appointed moderator. Soon after he reached the Narragansett camp, Captain Atherton of the Union arrived with twenty armed men ready to collect tribute at pistol point.

Roger's anger was magnificent. "I am betrayed by the four Colonies!" he cried to the Captain. "If your cause is so just, why do you come to a peaceful council meeting in guise of war? Why resort to trickery?"

In the end he persuaded Atherton that the debt was unjust and should be canceled. When Pessicus was told of this change of heart, there was great rejoicing around the campfire. The armed enemy was changed to a friend, and the good Captain joined

Roger in an appeal to John Winthrop. Between them they made the Union officials face the terrible consequences of stirring up a tribal war. For some time they ceased plotting to overthrow the powerful Narragansetts.

Massachusetts Puritans, however, were never at a loss for holy reasons to perform unchristian acts. Religious persecution there took a violent turn that year. It startled Providence out of concentrating on the wicked tangle William Harris had made of the land question.

At Chad Brown's house one afternoon, a constitutional committee was hard at work. Suddenly Thomas James burst into the room.

Stuttering with excitement, he cried, "A dire event hath happened in Massachusetts. Here is John Clark just come from there to tell you of it."

Clark looked like a man still in deep nervous shock. But he recited his tale with calm brevity. As the others knew, he had gone with two fellow Baptists from Newport to a village called Lynn in Massachusetts. There at the house of a friend they were holding Baptist services. Suddenly a constable knocked at the door with orders to arrest "the erroneous persons." The Newport men were marched first to a Puritan church service and then off to jail. At the court trial Governor Endicott himself appeared and said to John Clark, "You are worthy of death for your foul heresy." The heretics were sentenced to a fine or whipping. Clark, suddenly released, found that someone had paid his fine. One of the others also was freed. But the third Baptist, refusing to pay the fine, was publicly whipped and was still in a serious condition of health.

"What can we do," asked Clark in a desperate tone, "to protect ourselves from such violent interference? That Massachusetts hath no liberty of worship we know. That its churches and government are intertwined in authority we know. But punishment of men from another Colony is something new and to be dreaded."

Roger spent that evening writing a scathing letter to Governor Endicott. The whole Colony was stirred. Anger and helplessness and fear of the Union had now reached a climax. Within their midst was Coddington, bent on his career as dictator. In case of trouble, would he not join the foes of Providence Plantations?

Something must be done to save the Colony. A general meeting of citizens was called. There it was decided again to send agents to England to plead the cause of justice against William Coddington and the federated Colonies. Once more Roger was chosen to go. But this time John Clark and a secretary were to be sent also. When Roger hesitated to undertake the task, the government voted to pay him one hundred pounds for his last trip, a debt some seven years overdue. Even so he had to sell his beloved trading station in order to provide both for his own expenses and for his family.

When Roger learned that Mrs. Clark was going with her husband, he said to his wife, "Could I but take you with us, Mary, the sea would not look so wide, nor the months seem so long."

Bravely as ever she bade him good-by. This time Massachusetts dared not refuse to let the party sail from Boston harbor. It was November 1651 when the ship weighed anchor. Now they were going to a strange England, one ruled by Oliver Cromwell as

Captain General, assisted by a small and ghostly Parliament and by a few leaders whom Cromwell had chosen.

" 'Tis Sir Harry Vane, Lord of the Admiralty, whom I shall see first," Roger said to Clark. "He will understand that on the success of this mission hangs the whole future of our Colony."

14

THAT second mission for the Colony proved costly in time and effort. For two and a half years Roger worked, watched, and waited in London. So rapid were the changes in government, so uncertain was the final authority necessary to ratify the charter, that he was afraid to leave the city.

Between the Rump Parliament, under Sir Harry Vane's leadership, and the army, headed by Cromwell, a tug of war went on for more than a year. The army insisted that Parliament disband to make way for a new election of men representing the whole of England. Vane, fearing that the right men would not be chosen and alarmed by the danger of military rule, urged Parliament to hold on until reforms were put through.

In mid-April 1653 the climax came. With a company of soldiers at his back, Cromwell turned out Parliament by force. "Your hour has come!" he cried. "The Lord hath done with you!"

A constitutional convention was summoned and its work went on for months. But the reform program outlined was too severe both for Cromwell and for most property holders. Discouraged by the cross fire of criticism, the convention disbanded and tossed the reins of government over to the Lord General. He appointed a council of officers and under these auspices the year 1654 began.

Long before that time the old Parliamentary Council of State had dissolved Coddington's grant and restored the charter of 1644 to Providence Plantations. Official report of this action was carried back to the Colony by the man who served as secretary for the mission. Neither Williams nor Clark, however, thought it wise to leave then. But when Cromwell definitely took on the government in 1654, he assured Roger that the president of the officers' council would issue ratification of the charter, and the promise convinced Roger that at last he could go home with a free mind. Down he went into Lincolnshire to bid farewell to Sir Harry Vane, who was now a virtual prisoner on his own estate.

The Vanes were sad to part with their friend. Not only had they lived through many critical moments together, but also they shared the sorrowful knowledge that in England liberty was now a military prisoner.

One balmy spring evening as they sat together on the terrace, Lady Vane asked, "Mr. Williams, when you are again in Providence, what event in England's troubled days will you remember as the one which moved you most?"

He smiled. "The question bears reflection. Ofttimes noisy scenes, such as the day when the Lord General drove out Parliament, do sink down and a quieter thing seems more important."

As he spoke, he remembered absorbing talks with John Milton, now gone completely blind in service to the Council. They had exchanged views on politics, education, religion, and literature, and it was Milton who had urged Roger to write a pamphlet against the state church, called *The Hireling Ministry None of Christ's*.

228

Suddenly Roger's face lighted. "Perhaps I shall think most often of one late afternoon a year ago, madam, when many gentlemen at your house talked of whether Jews could live with Christians."

Ah, yes, Sir Harry also remembered the occasion. Oliver St. John had suddenly asked Roger in a voice which silenced all other talk, "Mr. Williams, would you accept as residents of your Colony people of the Jewish faith?"

Everyone had turned to Roger with a peculiar passion of interest. During the last year that question had rung in the ears of English liberals. Petitions had been sent to Parliament by European Jews asking permission to return to England.

Since the time of Edward First in the late 13th Century no Jew had been allowed to reside in the British Isles. But at this moment of struggle for religious tolerance, people of the Hebrew faith saw a chance for repeal of the exclusion act. Their petition stirred every sensitive conscience. But few thought it possible that Jews could be accepted in a Christian community. Intently Sir Harry's guests had hung upon Roger's answer to Oliver St. John.

It came prompt and clear. "Assuredly Jews would be welcome to our Colony. I doubt not we shall soon hear their knock upon our door. How could we refuse to open it? Sir, we believe in liberty of conscience as a principle for all."

"Ah," cried St. John triumphantly, "this good word must be repeated to Oliver Cromwell."

"Aye, let him read this!" Sir Harry Vane was holding up a well-worn pamphlet. "In *The Bloody Tenet* Mr. Williams has put the case right well in his preface. Listen, friends:

> *" ' 'Tis the will of God that a permission of*
> *the most Paganish, Jewish, Turkish or Anti-*
> *christian consciences and worships bee granted*
> *to all men in all Nations and Countries; and*
> *they are only to bee fought against with that*
> *Sword which is only (in Soule matters) able*
> *to conquer, to wit, the Sword of God's Spirit,*
> *the Word of God.' "*

For an exalted moment a vision of brotherhood held the company. Then a dry voice broke the spell. "Never will Presbyterians in Parliament pass a bill permitting Jewish citizens in our land!"

A disconsolate murmur of agreement was heard on all sides. But St. John squared his shoulders. "Mayhap there might be some way less emblazoned to the public than a bill of Parliament whereby a beginning might be made of friendliness to Jews. I shall take it up with Cromwell and shall report what Mr. Williams hath said."

As this scene unrolled before Roger, he bent upon his host and hostess a look of radiant hope. "From that evening's talk much may come. For Mr. St. John told me the Lord General believed a few Jewish families might be brought to England and settled quietly in London and in Oxford and nobody the wiser. Lord Cromwell said if some passed through the back door, others would follow and one day the exclusion act would be repealed. That will bring nearer the true fellowship of men preached by Jesus Christ."

Before Roger left Lincolnshire, Sir Harry Vane wrote for personal delivery a long letter to the General Court of Massachusetts. In it with tactful firmness he urged that leaders of the Colony cease from strife and persecution and devote themselves to the public good.

At the moment of farewell, Sir Harry said solemnly, "My friend, you go to achieve in Narragansett what here has been abandoned. Often have you said godliness and liberty cannot be upheld by the sword. Cromwell will fail. So, if I can aid you in making one spot on earth a place where Englishmen are free, I shall count it a boon."

During the seven weeks of the sea voyage those parting words sounded often in Roger's ears. Well he knew that freedom had yet to be won in the Colony of Providence and Rhode Island. Coddington had not accepted the ruling which deprived him of power. He had refused to turn over the statute books and paid no heed to the elections. Troubles with the Dutch, wrangling over land claims, and disobedience to officials kept affairs in confusion.

However, by last report sent to him in London, Roger knew that the party of law and order was supporting the central government. Serenely he gathered himself up to meet the quarrelsome, colorful characters who balked democracy on Narragansett Bay.

Armed with a special letter from Cromwell, he was landing in Boston. To his homesick eyes the New World seemed a vision of radiant beauty. Little gardens in the town were bright with flowers and the woods along the trail southward were splashed with delicate blooms of laurel, wild azalea, and fragrant, small roses.

Crowds of fellow citizens turned out to welcome back their representative. First at Seekonk and then at Providence they surged about him. Some were eager to hear news of England.

Others were still more eager to report the problems of the Colony. Patiently the traveler talked and listened. But the hours dragged until at last he had crossed his own threshold and was once more in the warm embrace of his family.

In astonishment he looked at his children. Mary and Freeborne were now young ladies with suitors begging for their hands. Marcy was fourteen and already versed in household arts. As for the boys, Providence, the eldest, was a tall youth of sixteen, Daniel was twelve, and even Joseph at ten had taken on a manly air.

It was plain how much the boys had missed their father. They pelted him with reports on the farm, boasted of their skill in fishing and sailing, chattered about the other youngsters in the town and about the Indians. But when Roger unpacked his boxes, the remarks his sons made gave him a shock.

"Didst thou bring home nought but books?" asked Daniel in disgust.

Providence picked up a pamphlet—one of John Milton's famous tracts—and said curiously, "What language might this be?"

Roger looked at him in horror. "My son, know you no word of Latin? 'Tis a fine thing to be good at swimming and to name the trees and plants of the forest. But there is a need for everyone to learn something out of books."

"My dear wife," he said when he and Mary were alone, "I have been too much away, too busy earning a livelihood and making a Colony. From this day forward I mean to look to the children's education."

Mary's eyes filled with loving laughter. "Aye, 'tis time. The Indians have been your children and the naughty men of Aquidneck. But indeed you have offspring of your own blood who need

you sorely."

With his usual energy Roger began a systematic
toring for the boys. They had lively minds and wer
be in the center of their father's attention. Before r
had passed the Cambridge Master of Arts was trying
children's benefit the educational experiments discussed
Milton.

Lessons had to be fitted in to the tutor's public task
gling the Colony's politics. In July a general assembly
As grievances were aired, it was evident that in each of
towns a strong minority opposed the policy of the central
ment. But the chief obstacle to union was the stubborn r
of William Coddington. His only concession was to invit
cial conference on the affairs of Rhode Island.

In August another assembly, this time held at Warwick
Roger Williams as Moderator. Things moved forward ther
charter of 1644 was formally reinstated. Articles of agreeme
a union were adopted and certain additions were made to the
of laws passed in 1651. These included the strict regulatic
liquor sales to the Indians and the exclusion of both French
Dutch traders from the Colony. Finally a court of election
chosen and when the votes were counted in September Willi;
had been made president of the Colony until the following M

He did not try to solve all the vexing problems at once. To l
Assistants he said, "We have law on our side and powerful frien
in England. Let us give Coddington and other rebels rope for th
hanging of ambition."

What could not wait was work for peace with the Indians. Racial distrust and tribal hatreds seemed more violent than ever. A

new sachem had grown great in the last decade. He was Ninigret of the Niantics. These fierce warriors, like their friends the Mohawks, were enemies of both red-skinned rivals and all white men, whether English or Dutch. Ninigret's quarrel with the Long Island tribes endangered trade along all the southern coast of New England.

In the heathen world things were always happening which seemed crimes to the colonists. Whether troubles should be smoothed out or punished by force of arms was the question constantly before New England leaders. The Union always inclined to punitive expeditions. Roger Williams ever sought to talk matters over with the sachems in conference, to discover the cause of disturbance, and uproot it by treaty and compromise. Although he acted alone, his influence with the Indians was tremendous.

During the fall of 1654 and the spring of 1655, this solitary peacemaker went the rounds of the tribes. Unarmed and fearless, he had a conference with Ninigret. With a happy sense of reunion he visited the Narragansett camp. Here he got the facts at first hand. Patiently he explained the situation in letters to the United Colonies and to John Winthrop. Ninigret had been outrageously betrayed by a group from the Long Island tribe. The Narragansetts lived always under the threat of invasion by the English Union.

A firm letter to the Massachusetts Bay Company recalled Cromwell's command that it cease disturbing the Narragansetts. Never once had that tribe drawn white blood. "All our families," wrote Roger, "have grown up in peace amongst them." He spoke of John Eliot of Massachusetts who had worked for many years to bring Christianity to the Indians. Then he added this sentence:

"Consider the paradox or clashings of these two, viz: the glorious conversion of the Indians in New England and the unnecessary wars and cruel distructions of the Indians in New England."

For a time it seemed as if all Roger's efforts were in vain. In the autumn of 1654 John Winthrop demanded vengeance against the Niantics. He claimed that on his farms near New London the tribe had killed a large and valuable herd of goats. Since there were other scores against the Niantics, the Union sent an armed force against them. So once again fear and hate filled the villages and forests. The militia killed a number of Indian warriors and drove others into the swamps, but many Englishmen also were lost in the campaign. After suffering great hardships as winter drew on, the troops at last took ship and sailed back home. Nothing had been accomplished and Union officials admitted that perhaps action had been too hasty.

Roger was ready to make use of this changed mood. He had been working on the same affair in his own way. Inviting all the sachems of the Niantic and Narragansett tribes, he held an enormous conference at Warwick. Some sixty armed warriors who came with the chiefs struck terror to the hearts of the town's timid citizens. But Roger delighted in the occasion. At last he was getting at the truth and showing the natives that one Englishman, at least, loved them enough to be fair.

When all was over and the good-bys were said, Roger went to rest at the house of Samuel Gorton. In the latter years of struggle the two men had become good friends. Stretched out on the settle, with a glass of mulled wine to warm him, the mediator reported the conference to his host.

"What actually happened to cause the Union's murderous campaign shall be reported to Mr. Winthrop this very night. Indians have died and white men have suffered, Mr. Gorton, because four goats were slain. Four!" A note of despairing amusement crept into his voice. "The Niantics admit the four. But the herd was stolen by English settlers trusted by Winthrop and sold to Dutch traders. Indians are ever blamed for all misdeeds by men who trouble not to find the facts. They feel no kinship with the poor heathen. Oh, 'tis enough to make the angels weep."

Gorton sighed sympathetically. "Aye, Mr. Williams. Had a conference been called at once, the Union's armed force would never have been sent."

The Warwick meeting, however, was in time to prevent another disaster. Frankly the Narragansetts discussed their deadly feud with a Dutch trader. He had robbed the grave of an Indian princess, the sister of Pessicus, and the sachems were thirsting for vengeance.

Roger said the matter should be handled by due process of law. As agent of the tribe, he could attach the goods and credit of the Dutchman. By this means the thief could be fined and forced to return the stolen treasures. "Murder heals no wrong and pleases no good god," said the counselor. The Narragansetts listened to their true friend of many years. Placing the affair in his hands, they promised to keep the peace.

A letter from England awaited Roger's return from Warwick. It brought hope to all lovers of liberty. During the previous year the nation had had a Parliament representing all but Royalists.

For the first time in history men from Scotland and Ireland sat with English members. But because grants of money were delayed, some feared that Cromwell would lose patience with the House. Peace had been made with Holland, but the fleet was about to turn its guns on Spanish shipping.

Gravely the Williams boys listened to this report. Suddenly Daniel said, "Father, since others look to you, why cannot you put down the rebels in this Colony? I'll warrant the Lord Protector would stamp out disorders here."

His father's eyes flashed with sudden anger. Most adults were like this child. They wanted results no matter what the means, and thought patience was weakness. Yet he could not deny something must be done. Discontent had mounted to open defiance of the government. Pacifists and anarchists were leading in revolt all those who disliked control of any kind. Attempts were being made to overturn procedure in the courts.

Even the rich conservative, Thomas Olney, had become a rebel. The lawless deals he had made in land, urged on by William Harris, had undermined his respect for orderly procedure. Roger suspected the change in him, but not the lengths to which he was prepared to go.

Suddenly one day as Roger was walking along the Pequot trail he met a company of armed men led by Thomas Olney. They had to halt to let him pass. In astonishment Roger asked the meaning of this display of force.

Olney answered in an insolent tone, "We are volunteer militia, training to defend our properties and persons."

"From what enemies, Mr. Olney?" asked his challenger gravely. "Indian threat is allayed. The regular militia is at hand.

I fear there is behind this company some purpose different from the common defense."

"Think what you must, Mr. President," replied Olney coolly and barked out, "Forward, men!"

Even before the winter of 1655, rioting occurred in Warwick, Providence, and Newport. Every attempt of officers to enforce the law was resisted. Coddington still acted as governor of Rhode Island. William Harris led bands of armed men through the towns, shouting that they did not mean to have a charter imposed upon them nor a rule of fools.

After one of these noisy demonstrations on the green, Thomas James drew Roger into his house. "What causes decent men to oppose a democratic government voted by the majority?" he asked.

"They fear some loss of independence," was the thoughtful answer. "You see, Mr. James, we have talked much about the rights of man, but all too little of the discipline and sacrifice needed for the common good. I must try to make such matters clear."

That very night he wrote out a little lesson for the townsmen.

"There goes many a ship to sea, with many hundred souls in one ship, whose weal and woe is common, and is a true picture of a commonwealth, or human habitation or society.

"It hath fallen out sometimes, that both papists and protestants, Jews and Turks, may be embarked in one ship; upon which supposal I affirm, that all the liberty of conscience, that I ever pleaded for, turns upon these two

hinges—that none of the papists, protestants, Jews or Turks, be forced to come to the ship's prayers or worship, nor compelled from their own particular prayers or worship, if they practise any.

"I further add, that I never denied, that notwithstanding this liberty, the commander of this ship ought to command the ship's course, yea, and also command that justice, peace and sobriety, be kept and practised, both among the seamen and all the passengers.

"If any of the seamen refuse to perform their services or passengers to pay their freight; if any refuse to help in person or purse, towards the common charges of defence; if any refuse to obey the common laws and orders of the ship, concerning the common peace and preservation; if any shall mutiny and rise up against their commanders and officers; if any should preach or write that there ought to be no commanders and officers, no laws nor orders, nor corrections, nor punishments;—I say, I never denied, but in such cases, whatever is pretended, the commander or commanders may judge, resist, compel and punish such transgressors, according to their deserts and merits.

"This if seriously and honestly minded, may, if it so please the Father of lights, let in

some light to such as willingly shut not the eyes."

Roger's message, passed from town to town, did let in light. No one could deny the sense of this instruction. Followers of the rebel leaders fell away and told others it was necessary to keep the common peace. Volunteers responded when armed aid was summoned to quell riots. Presently William Harris was arrested under a charge of rebellion and kept a prisoner until his trial before the March Court. When the Assembly met in May 1655, three other men, including Thomas Olney, were found guilty of disorder.

Having made this display of firmness, the leader swung toward mercy. He pled with the Assembly to dismiss the rebels with a warning. Chosen president once more, Roger set to work with full vigor to strengthen the central government and tighten authority. A glance at his program shows how wisely he dealt with the problems of those early days.

(1) Every new resident must swear allegiance to the government of England.

(2) The central government was to be financed by special funds and was no longer to depend on contributions by the towns.

(3) Tax collectors were appointed. Wages fixed for state officers and jurymen.

(4) Circuit Courts with quarterly meetings were organized. With two juries and town courts set up and penalties fixed for refusal to aid judges and jurymen, a strict control over lawbreakers was assured.

(5) Penalties were increased for illegal sale of liquor and for other misdemeanors and crimes.

(6) Each town was ordered to provide a public tavern.

(7) Warwick and Newport were each ordered to build a prison. Portsmouth and Providence must set up stocks and a cage for prisoners.

Order was fairly well restored now. Neither the central government nor the courts had further opposition. Yet two huge obstacles stood in the way of progress. William Coddington still claimed his authority. Massachusetts kept its official protection over the Pawtuxet families and the Shawomet Indians, who continued to give Warwick infinite trouble.

One day, when for the twentieth time a group of the Colony officials was discussing means to solve both problems, one of them said impatiently, "Why do we not order the militia to turn Mr. Coddington out? Then we shall be faced only with the Bay Company."

"No, no, no! Never that!" Roger's voice trembled with urgency. "Let us profit by the dire events in our native land. We must use persuasion and legal means, not force!"

His words had weight. No lover of liberty in America had heard unmoved the news from England that summer. In January 1655 Cromwell had abruptly dismissed Parliament. Now a sword hung over the land. It was divided into ten military districts. The Council of State consisted only of officers and the Lord Protector ruled supreme.

Strangely enough this violent change of authority helped Providence Plantations to dislodge William Coddington from his mythical governorship. The Newport fanatic at last realized his case was hopeless. The friends in England who had helped him into his false position had either died or had been imprisoned as enemies of Cromwell. His followers in Rhode Island had swung to the support of the central government. By March 1656 Coddington was ready to give allegiance to the laws of the Colony and the Lord Protector. He turned the statute books over to the executives and paid his fine for keeping them illegally. In return, the town clerk at the Assembly's order cut from the record certain statements hostile to the charter's prime enemy.

With renewed hope Roger then made a fresh effort to reach the conscience of Massachusetts. So far his missives had had no answer. But in May of that year he wrote a letter to Governor Endicott which was a triumph of diplomacy. Gently he reminded him of the orders from England that the Colony should cease persecuting the citizens of Warwick. This time a prompt reply was returned. Mr. Williams was invited up to Boston for a conference.

When that news reached Warwick, the town held a meeting. Samuel Gorton himself rode over to tell Roger the action taken by the citizens.

"We lack not gratitude for your efforts," said he, "and have voted expenses for your trip to Boston."

Roger's eyes opened wide. Never had the cost of any of his journeys in the Colony's behalf been fully paid, certainly not in advance. As he expressed warm thanks, he marveled at the change in the individual before him. Once Gorton was the gadfly of the region. Now he was gift-bearer to the defender of order.

"Mr. Williams," said the visitor, counting out a little pile of coins, "Warwick sends you these forty shillings. Also when you start forth, you will find in our town a horse ready to be loaned you. And look you here!" He unwrapped a package with intense pride. "This is a pair of breeches for your Indian servant and a shilling for his food."

To hide his helpless laughter Roger held up the gift full length before his face. In a choking voice he said, "Faith, you have forgot nothing, Mr. Gorton. Served by an Indian in these fine breeches, I am sure to win the case for Warwick."

In the end he did. His eloquent review of the stormy history of Warwick and Pawtuxet, his re-reading of the State Council's orders, made a strong impression upon Boston's magistrates. They never had had legal grounds for protecting the unruly dwellers of Pawtuxet. A courteous promise was made to take the matter up in the light now turned upon it. It required two years longer for the Bay Company to come to its decision. But in 1658, Massachusetts officially and finally withdrew all claim to authority over any lands within the territory of Providence Plantations and Rhode Island.

Some two months after that Boston conference, the General Assembly met. Earnest democrats passed resolutions that none of the laws made by the central government be obstructed. Roger Williams, again elected president the previous year, then read a letter from the Lord Protector.

Addressing himself to "Our trusty and well beloved president, assistants and inhabitants of Providence Plantations," Cromwell said, "You are to proceed in your government according to the tenor of your charter formerly granted . . . taking care of the peace and safety of these plantations." He signed the message, "your very loving friend, Oliver P."

In the hush that followed the reading, the members reflected upon those clear instructions. Then Thomas James arose.

"Mr. President and fellow citizens, in the spirit of such plain orders from England's ruler I do make this proposal. Let all leaders of rebel groups, all who are responsible for disorders here, from this time forward be sent to England at their own expense to stand trial there before the authorities they have disobeyed."

Roger's glance shifted from William Harris to Coddington and on to others who had defied the government. Each man looked startled and abashed. None of them dared protest.

"Question! Question!" shouted voices from every side. When the question was put, it was voted by a huge majority.

A great wave of thankfulness swept over the man in the president's chair. His patience had been justified. For it was the day by day experience of the benefits of democratic government which had built up public opinion on the side of law and order. Men were convinced that was what worked best. After this, if force had to be used, the majority of citizens would be behind it. Many different men had held office and so knowledge of the problems of government had become widespread. At last in this society formed on Narragansett Bay the average citizen had come to understand not only his common rights but his common duties.

Quite another human principle came to the fore that year. Late in the autumn, rumors from Boston ran swift as grass fire through the Colony. It seemed that members of a new religious sect had landed in Massachusetts only to find themselves treated like malefactors.

A delegation from the four towns appeared at the door of Roger

Williams' house one day. The spokesman said, "Sir, we would consult you about these new victims of persecution in our neighbor Colony. Do you know aught about them? They are called Quakers."

Like everyone else, Roger had heard what was happening in Boston. Men and women of that faith were being imprisoned, whipped, and threatened with exile or deportation to England. He shared the indignation sweeping through the Colony. Not a single member of it had ever seen a Quaker, with the exception of himself.

"Yes," he said after he had seated his visitors about the fire, "I have seen Quakers in London, heard them preach, studied their beliefs. George Fox is their leader. Many points of the doctrine seem to me false and without base. But what I most dislike is their noisy way of fixing attention on themselves. They interrupt meetings in other churches, go shouting through the streets, and otherwise behave unseemly."

In astonishment the delegation looked at the speaker. One man from Warwick said, "Mr. Gorton doth wish to open our town to these folk when they be sent from our harsh neighbor Colony. You would oppose that, I surmise, Mr. Williams?"

"Oppose it?" It was Roger's turn to stare. "Nay. 'Tis our plain duty to give them refuge. Boston's treatment of Quakers sickens my heart. Because I like not their preaching nor their deeds is not to say we should turn from their necessity. Let them come and let them preach. Should they disturb our peace, we may reprove them on civil grounds."

News of this interview was reported in every town. Gorton sent secret word to Massachusetts that the persecuted sect might come to Warwick. A few months later a number of Quakers settled in Warwick and in Newport. Quietly received, allowed to make converts if they could, few of these individuals gave any trouble. When their doctrines were divorced from the hysterical behavior characteristic of the sect in those far-off days, the beauty of the teaching became plain to all. The accent they put on freedom of conscience, on love of humanity, and on peace was in harmony with the general ideals of the Colony.

In 1657 Benedict Arnold had been elected president. The egotism and ambition of this young man had not inspired trust in the heart of Roger Williams. Therefore it was with some fear of contest ahead that he answered the president's summons to a conference one afternoon.

"I would consult you on this affair of the Quakers, Mr. Williams," said Arnold. "Last week I received a strange message from the magistrates of Massachusetts. They boldly presume to demand that we receive not in our midst any members of this sect."

The man who had battled half a lifetime for liberty of conscience felt a wild anger seething in his blood. How dared the Bay send such a message? By a strong effort of the will he gave no sign and sat in silence, waiting. What did this forceful young man think—that was what he wanted to know. Arnold had once placed himself under the protection of Massachusetts. Would he yield to its demands now? Gently he asked if the president had framed a reply.

"That I have, Mr. Williams. For some reason I wished you to see it before submitting the same to my Assistants." From the drawer of a bureau he took a page of writing and handed it to his companion.

From the very first paragraph Roger experienced a deep and joyous astonishment. Temperate, dignified, and firm was the writer's refusal to consider in any way the outrageous request of the neighbor Colony. Making no mention of Quakers by name he said:

> *"We have no law among us, whereby to punish any for only declaring by words theire mindes and understandings concerning the things and ways of God."*

It was as if Roger had received some personal reward. Here was a man ruthlessly selfish in material gain. Yet he was ready to prove true devotion to the principle on which Providence Plantations had been founded. Arnold's stand made it certain that even to the unruly minority of the Colony absolute religious liberty was a necessity.

"Mr. Arnold, no answer could be better." Quietly Roger laid down the paper. "Your words are the more piercing because they are free from anger." He was touched to see how his praise lighted the hard young face.

After a moment Benedict said, "None the less I am certain our message will anger officials of the Bay Company. This Colony will pay for such resistance."

He was right. Upon receipt of the letter, Boston authorities promptly passed edicts refusing facilities for trade and export to Providence Plantations. They called their neighbor "The sewer of New England" and the "State of Confusion." But neither mean epithets nor vengeful measures influenced the despised Colony. As news of Quaker persecution grew more distressing, as mutilated victims staggered across the borders of Massachusetts, eagerness to help them only increased.

It was a joyous surprise to find that the Colonies on the Connecticut River and the coast did not follow Massachusetts' example. Other members of the Union punished violent Quakers only by fines and reproof. Writing to congratulate John Winthrop on this moderation, Roger said that the community which treated the sect with friendly indifference had no trouble with it.

Yet the gentle tone of that letter disguised the writer's real feelings on the matter. The very day he sent it off Roger gathered his children about him for a private word.

"Be proud of your Colony, my children!" said he. "We alone have protested these terrible deeds against Christian men and women."

By 1658 Massachusetts had passed a death penalty for all Quakers found within its territory. That edict aroused a longing for martyrdom in many impassioned members of the group. They were determined to return from safe refuge and preach their doctrine in defiance of death. To the horror of all her fellow citizens on Rhode Island, Mary Dyer, a converted Quaker, was one of the victims of the hangman.

Deeper and deeper grew the dark clouds of intolerance over the Bay Colony. But even as citizens of the four Narragansett towns watched them gather, they themselves received from a new quarter a sharp challenge to their ideals.

Roger knew it was coming. He had heard reports from New Amsterdam and from Dutch traders along the coast that a new migration of persecuted people had begun. These were Jewish refugees. Ousted by Spain, a group of them had made their way to South America. But that was Spanish soil and they were at once put on a ship to be dumped on the North American coast within New Netherlands. The Dutch in America had joined in the ill-treatment and forcible exile of Quakers. Now they refused to receive this group of Jews.

Up from Newport spread news one long-remembered day in 1658. A ship had landed fifteen Jewish families. They had been kindly received and given food and shelter. But would the Colony keep them? Every tongue in Providence was wagging over the problem.

From the first, Roger serenely took the stand that there was no question about it. From him the conviction spread. As soon as his work permitted, he sailed down to Newport to meet the refugees and bid them welcome. When he did so, he delighted both the newcomers and the citizens of the town because he could converse with them in Dutch.

Before he started home, he said to William Coddington, "These will be sturdy, loyal citizens. You are honored to be the first to receive them. But 'tis my belief that Portsmouth and Providence will soon be welcoming other members of this race." A prediction that came true!

All the way back across Narragansett Bay Roger was sunk in deep reflection. How well he remembered the discussions he had once held on the subject of Jewish immigration with Oliver Cromwell. As Roger shifted the rudder to tack against the wind, he heard again the grinding voice and met the impenetrable gaze of the full-lidded eyes.

There was a reason for the vividness of these memories. For that day he had heard of the Lord Protector's death. In the wide silence between sea and sky Roger pondered the meaning of the leader's strange destiny. A God-fearing man, made dictator by no plan of his own, Cromwell had left England better organized than ever before. He had raised the country's world prestige to new heights by the might of English arms on land and sea. Yet in the end he had had to govern by the rule of force alone a sullen people who once with eager hands held high the torch of liberty.

And now what would happen? Would young King Charles Second be called to the throne? If so, would he ratify the charter of the democratic Colony on Narragansett Bay? A charter granted by the men who slew his father!

Somehow Roger found no urgency in these questions. In a general way he trusted the future. Here along the coast of America a new and vital way of life was taking root. It was impossible to believe that the mother country would crush it down. In only a little more than twenty years, men of Providence Plantations had learned much about self-government. Liberty of conscience had become an unshakable conviction. Behind these two bulwarks, the individual was free from dictation by the state.

Yet the clear eyes of this political philosopher held no illusions. He knew that although the democratic government might endure, the economic struggle was likely to be fierce and ruthless. That very day when he reached Providence he first put in words these doubts which long afterwards were set down in a letter to a Connecticut official.

Eager to talk to somebody about Cromwell's death, he stopped in at the house of his friend, Thomas James. James was frankly glad the autocrat of the motherland had passed from power. Nobody need fear the future, said he. The Colony had never been so firm and free and unified.

"True, Mr. James," said Roger. "My only lack of ease comes from watching the depraved appetite for land increasing here. Land in this wilderness! Men act as if great portions of woods and empty meadows meant as much to them as food and water to thirsty seamen after a long and starving passage. Ah, sir, this is one of the gods of New England which the Eternal will destroy and famish!"

James listened with admiration for his friend's capacity to hate evil. "'Tis true. Foul deeds have already been done for gain by ambitious fools amongst us and William Harris heads the list. Not yet have we seen an end to this evil."

After a moment's silence, James got up and went to a bureau in a corner of the room. Over his shoulder he said, "Yet in some things, Mr. Williams, this Colony hath held up hope of a better society. Do you remember the letter you sent not so long ago to our noble friend, Sir Harry Vane? Gregory Dexter was town clerk then and he made a copy of it for me. Let me read a passage to cheer your spirits."

Seating himself again, he read from the letter which was destined to be quoted by every historian of the period.

> "... *We have long drunk of the cup of as great liberties as any people that we can hear of under the whole heaven. We have not only long been free (together with all New England) from the iron yoke of wolfish bishops,*

*and their popish ceremonies, but we have sitten
quiet and dry from the streams of blood spilt
by that war in our native country.*

*"We have not felt the new chains of the
Presbyterian tyrants, nor in this colony have
we been consumed with the over-zealous fire
of the (so-called) godly christian magistrates.
Sir, we have not known what an exise means;
we have almost forgotten what tithes are, yea
or taxes either, to church or commonwealth."*

Looking up from the page, James met the eyes of his companion—the lonely eyes of a man who had gazed into far distance.

"Thank you, my friend," murmured Roger. He leaned back against the settle. Well he knew that at home a dozen duties claimed him. But it was good for a moment to sit in silence and reflect upon the sources of goodness which made human progress possible.

At last he said, " 'Twas well to read the letter. At least it renews in us what we do really know. There is a spirit of liberty in this little Colony. Thank God for that!"

15

AMERICANS are just beginning to realize what Roger Williams did for us. Without him, the New World would not have been new, for he brought to it an irresistible passion for freedom which started us on our way.

He won the great battle for religious freedom. To do so he had to strive on both sides of the ocean. In America he founded a state based on liberty of conscience. In England his written and spoken words made minds tingle with the electricity of brave ideas. In a rush of healthy shame persecution was outlawed. Colonies began to be started in a more liberal spirit and slowly the belief spread that religion and government should be separate. For this reason the United States never had a national church and all faiths have been welcomed here.

The second contribution of this pioneer was to create the first truly democratic government. Theories pointing that way had been growing in popularity. But Williams stated them with breath-taking courage:

> "Governmental agencies have not the least inch of civil power but what is measured out to them from the free consent of the whole."

Then he put the principle into practice and proved that a government which was the instrument of the people would actually work.

By sheer genius he devised a sound and flexible plan for a self-ruled society. He made citizens of his colony the envy of all who lived under the thumb of theocracies, royal governors, and arbitrary proprietors. The moment the Thirteen States declared independence of England, each of them adopted some form of democratic organization. Naturally the Constitutional Convention framed a similar plan for the nation.

Political power and liberty of thought as possessions of the people were novelties three hundred years ago. True, ever since the Reformation thinkers of the Western World had been discussing such possibilities. But Williams was the first to outline the *rights of man*. He did so in his pamphlets and in the preamble to the original constitution of Rhode Island. Never before on earth had these rights been embodied in an actual government.

Loyalty to this tradition met its great test in 1788. When the citizens of the state were presented the Constitution in that year, they refused to accept it until Congress had passed the Bill of Rights. Theirs was a powerful influence for the protection of our whole people.

As long as Roger Williams lived—and he lived to be an old man—he himself *was* the spirit of liberty in America. With unflagging energy, patience, and love of all living creatures, he worked to realize his dream of fellowship. Because he created a practical government of the people, organized a system of courts, and wrote a just penal code; because, after having done so, he could train men to use these tools, he proved himself one of the greatest statesmen who ever lived.

The power of this leader was not cut off by death. He belongs to our present and our future. The man who called himself a Seeker opened up new vistas to the religious impulse. He showed narrow-minded fanatics of all time that the important factor in a man's life is direct contact with the Spiritual World. Belonging to a church is no substitute for applying the principles of religion to life itself.

Roger Williams' life illustrates what has to be done if religion is to come true on earth. How to apply it to all relationships, all tasks and duties, is made very clear by this man's activities. They throw light on the most gripping problems of the immediate future.

Foremost among them is race prejudice. What is race prejudice? It is an unreasoning and unloving attitude toward a whole group of people born into the world as members of a certain race. Prejudice against a race is based on a feeling of superiority.

Roger Williams saw it operating in New England against the Indians. Englishmen considered them inferior. Certainly in education, opportunity, and the kind of social experience we call civilization, the natives were no match for the immigrants. But white superiority expressed itself by taking every possible advantage of the redskins. Land was stolen from them—hundreds of acres at a clip. Traders exchanged worthless gewgaws for valuable furs. Continual sale of liquor to the tribes undermined their morale in a single generation. Colonial officials really preferred military expeditions to arbitration when trouble with a tribe arose, for it gave them a chance to seize more land and power.

While superiority was thus at work, John Eliot of Massachusetts was translating the Bible into the Indian language and was boasting of converting savages to Christianity. Churchmen in London and New England alike were very proud of this work. It was a beautiful screen for the wickedness of English and Dutch officials in their policy toward the natives.

Like a white silhouette on a black page, the attitude of Roger Williams towards the Indians stands out in contrast to that of other leaders.

To him, superior endowment and worldly advantage came by Heaven's Grace. They carried an obligation to love and understand all who were less fortunate. To fulfill that obligation brings humility. For the moment one begins to love and understand others, their own superior virtues appear. Roger's *Key into the Language of America* gave Englishmen for the first time some notion of the admirable traits of the Indians.

> *"I could never discern that excess of scandalous sins amongst them which Europe aboundeth with. Drunkenness and gluttony generally they knew not what sinnes they be; and although they have not so much to restrain them both in respect of a knowledge of God, and the laws of men, as the English have, yet a man shall never hear of such amongst them as robberies, murthers, adulteries, etc., as amongst the English."*

258

Of their hospitality, Williams said:

> *"Whomsoever cometh in when they are eating, they offer them to eat of that which they have, though but little enough prepared for themselves. . . . Many a time and at all times in the night, as I have fallen in travel upon their houses, when nothing hath been ready, have themselves and their wives risen to prepare me some refreshing. It is a strange truth that a man shall generally find more free entertainment and refreshing amongst these Barbarians than amongst thousands that call themselves Christians."*

He admired the strength and cleverness of the Indians. He said they were "joyful in travel" and inventive about household tools and decorations. To him, their tribal family life had much beauty of affection and of custom. He watched their games, their ceremonies and conferences. Affection without tinge of sentimentality led him to fair judgment of this people. He judged them just as he did Englishmen. Some were tricky, some had an unfailing sense of honor.

After learning much about their religion, which included thirty-seven gods, he came to the conclusion that converting Indians to Christianity was possible in only one way. It wasn't by baptism or ritual or Sabbath laws or teaching prayers by rote. Only if a white man himself practiced his beliefs with passionate conviction could he make any impression upon a savage. So long as the English and Dutch failed to apply to Indians the love, mercy, and justice taught by their religion, talk of conversion was hypocrisy and illusion.

To do as you would be done by—that was Roger's simple rule. Because he never ceased to follow it, he was the trusted friend of all the tribes. He returned their hospitality, sold them useful articles only, paid in wampum or services for land, and at all times told them the truth. In order to prevent destructive wars he traveled hundreds of miles, risked his life, argued and planned.

All these things he did because he really cared for the good of native Americans. He hoped that somehow the two races might learn to share life together in the wilderness. How little he felt the superiority of the white man appears in this quaint verse from *Key into the Language of America:*

> *"When Indians hear the horrid filth*
> *Of Irish, Englishmen*
> *The horrid oaths and murders hate*
> *Thus say the Indians then:*

> *"We wear no clothes, have many gods*
> *And yet our sins are less.*
> *You are barbarians, pagans wild,*
> *Your land's the wilderness.*

> *"Oft have I heard the Indians say*
> *These English will deceive us.*
> *Of all that's ours, our lands and lives,*
> *In the end they will bereave us."*

Every word and act of Roger Williams in dealing with the Indians should be studied by Americans today. In this land are many nationalities, many races. All of us have to learn to live and work together. With humor, patience, and mutual respect we, too, may hope that all the races on this continent can some day share life here on equal terms. Williams showed us the way. He knew that good and bad persons can be found in every race. His example shows that it is the duty of every individual to work actively against racial prejudice wherever it blazes out.

To Roger Williams, Jews were people of an ancient religion, not a separate race. When the question of admitting Jews to Rhode Island came up, it seemed to him no different from the question of welcoming Quakers. And there could be but one answer to it. Either one believed in the *principle* of liberty of conscience or one didn't. Believers had to apply the principle to all people everywhere.

Williams hated backward ideas and selfishness wherever he found them. He saw no difference between the trickery of Uncas, the Mohegan, and that of the notable members of the Massachusetts General Court, who tried by forgery to steal Narragansett territory. An individual must be judged, not by race or color, but by what he himself is—that was his rule. It holds good today.

Another reason why Roger Williams belongs to our day and to the future is very different in character. It concerns the problems of wealth and trade. They loom before the whole world—enormous, confused, unsolved. In Roger's primitive society no such complexities appeared. But they were foreshadowed. Now, as then, human thought about money-making enterprises is the important factor in progress. And the founder of the colony which came to be called Rhode Island offered such far-reaching suggestions that we haven't yet grown up to them.

First of all, modern business has become tangled up with government. Many men believe this is one of the main causes of war. The workers and the farmers, the artists and the scientists around the globe do not wish to fight one another. But when powerful groups, representing invested capital, succeed in getting special favors from a government, that nation is soon involved in a struggle for territory, for oil fields, airports, mines, and plantations in the far corners of the earth.

Compared to this mighty clash of interests in modern times, the colonial issues in the 17th Century seem no more intense than a chess game. Yet they offer in miniature a clear picture of the unholy alliance between government and private power.

In Connecticut and Massachusetts the government was composed of landowners, capitalists, and industrial magnates of fishing, shipping, and lumber interests. They wanted to dominate the entire Narragansett Bay region. With no warrant from the people they governed, these officials used every possible means to that end. Rhode Island out-maneuvered them, thanks to its leader. But their policy finally brought about King Philip's War. That was the bitterest cup ever pressed to the lips of the one true friend of the Indians. Tribal power was then destroyed and the English could expand at will.

Roger Williams judged New England politics for what they were. In his philosophy there was no imperialism. Certainly he was sure the state ought not to go into business. He rejoiced when Plymouth gave up its attempt to own and operate enterprises as a communal effort. Nothing like that was ever tried in Providence

Plantations. There men were free to use talent, invention, and energy for the creation of wealth—*provided the common welfare was preserved!*

An instance of what this safeguard meant is Roger's action when he was president of the Colony in 1655. Through his influence the Assembly then passed measures to control the liquor trade. Chief among these was a law prohibiting a dealer from selling more than half a pint of liquor to an Indian. Drunken savages were a source of grave peril to the community.

The main duties of the government to its people, as Williams framed them, were positive. First on the list was defense of citizens. Even the original handful of settlers took turns as guards to prevent fires and keep off human and animal marauders. Later the central government was empowered to settle quarrels at home and abroad by arbitration. If that means failed, the militia was ready to act. Threat of riots among headstrong townfolk or of invasion by the Dutch or by hostile Indians was met by the armed guard.

In the primitive annals of the Colony we also find a hint of modern provision for social security. In 1650 Williams made an eloquent plea to the Assembly for an allowance to an orphaned girl, "distracted" because a penniless condition was forcing her into a miserable marriage.

An instrument for common, equal rights—that was what government should be, according to this statesman. If today, governments the world over were devoted only to the equal rights of their people, there would be far less danger of bureaucracy and of the lobbying for special privilege which leads to war.

Since the dawn of time the most basic of all privilege is private ownership of land. Land, of course, is in a class by itself. Men do not invent it as they invent machines. Age-old processes of nature created the forests, the fertile fields, and all the buried treasures of coal, metals, minerals, and oil. Who ought to possess this gift of nature on which civilization depends?

Roger Williams never stated that land should be commonly owned. But we do know that he believed it ought to be shared. He set the example by practically giving away huge tracts of territory ceded to him by the Narragansetts. As long as he lived he made it possible, by standing off the opposition of certain mean-minded townsmen, for newcomers to get land in Providence, and he insisted on grants of twenty-five acres to poor men. These also had, by Roger's insistence, a right in public pasture meadows. When he bought Prudence Island from old Canonicus, he shared it with John Winthrop for the purpose of raising goats.

All his transactions show a powerful conviction that man's right to land depends on *use*. Private ownership worked no ill so long as it meant merely the erection of homes, mills, trading stations, and the development of farms. But in that untamed wilderness soon appeared the disease which has undermined our economy—land speculation. This accounts in large part today for bankrupt cities, poor housing, high rents, and unfair distribution of wealth. Buy land and hold it idle until increase of population or some other change makes it very desirable; then sell or rent it for huge sums—that is the practice which imperils economic health.

In Providence Plantations a group of ambitious men started such operations soon after they arrived. It was the more disheartening to the founder of the Colony because when he accepted these individuals as residents of the town, all but one was penniless. For years Roger battled with this evil. He knew it as the greatest enemy to the success of his experiment in democracy. To John Winthrop he wrote:

> *"I fear the common Trinities of the world,*
> *(Profit, Preferment, Pleasure) will here be the*
> tri omnia, *as in all the world beside . . ."*

How can the deeply rooted maladies of speculation and private ownership in land be overcome? Not easily. Any people determined on a cure must find a genius to devise a method of relief and then be ready for long, resolute effort. Yet what is impossible? Three hundred years ago one man's unique combination of statecraft and devotion to his fellows achieved a democracy for the first time. In proving that a great conviction can be practically demonstrated, Williams held up a light which might today flood the darkest corners of the world.

That conviction was the very one which inspired the great slogan of the French Revolution. Williams tried to apply in a living way the same threefold principle—liberty of thought and worship, equality in the political sphere and—what about fraternity? At least he had the courage to raise that still unanswered question—how can a feeling of brotherhood modify the tigerish competition in business and industry without smothering individual enterprise?

How strange it is that only lately we have begun to take the measure of such a leader! It is partly his own fault. Roger Williams had a kind of modesty we hardly understand in this day of glaring publicity. Like the architect of the Parthenon and the sculptors of the marvelous figures on the cathedral of Chartres, this man was only interested in results. He wanted to strip religion of hate and prejudice and ignorance. His aim was to build a free society. What did he care about personal credit? Future fame meant nothing to him.

There was another reason why we haven't known him. Nobody living in America during his lifetime had the ability to appreciate him. His enemies called him "divinely mad," said he was a "firebrand" and a "windmill blown about by crazy ideas." Even those who loved him couldn't estimate what he accomplished. They handed down a radiant tradition of his friendship with the Indians and of his readiness to protect the persecuted. But they couldn't recognize his genius.

That was natural. There is nothing startlingly dramatic about the slow work of molding a new world. What he wanted was to teach men to take responsibility for a healthy social life. Therefore, when he held office, made speeches, wrote pamphlets, and created a constitution, it was only in order to advance an idea or push forward other leaders. When the enterprise began to go, few remembered how it started. But today we are becoming keenly conscious of the meaning of America. Young and old grope through modern material success to find the clean, daylit spaces where the seeds of liberty were planted. Hard at work there, all by himself, we have discovered the founder of Rhode Island.

American history offers no more thrilling episode than the lone journey of Roger Williams. He set forth on a dangerous path into the unknown. It led to freedom for mankind. He didn't reach the goal, but he never faltered. And he blazed the trail!